SELF DEFENSE
for
NATURE LOVERS

HANDLING DANGEROUS SITUATIONS WITH WILD CRITTERS

Mike Lapinski

SELF DEFENSE
for
NATURE LOVERS

HANDLING DANGEROUS SITUATIONS WITH WILD CRITTERS

Mike Lapinski

Copyright 1998 by Mike Lapinski

ISBN 0-912299-77-0

Library of Congress Catalog Card Number 98-61498

Published in the United States of America

Wisdom Is Better Than Strength

This book was written from the author's personal experiences, and research, and represents his opinions on ways one can avoid or stop an animal attack. However, neither this book nor any other can ensure your safety because wild creatures are unpredictable; thus, it is not intended as the final word on potentially dangerous encounters with wild critters. Ultimately, in those situations, you must rely upon yourself.

Sound judgement and prudence are the most important assets for any nature lover. Remember, wisdom is better than strength. And realize that you take upon yourself the responsibility for how you respond on those occasions when your safety, or that of others, might depend upon how you handle the situation.

STONEYDALE PRESS PUBLISHING COMPANY
523 Main Street • P.O. Box 188
Stevensville, Montana 59870
Phone: 406-777-2729

Table of Contents

Cover Photo Credits: Mountain Lion and Bear by Mike Lapinski, Rattlesnake by Gary Holmes, Black Widow Spider by John Reid.

DEDICATION

This book is dedicated to my wife, Aggie.

After reading in the local newspaper that a mountain lion had mauled and nearly killed six-year-old Dante Swallow, who was a soccer teammate of our grandson, Thomas, Aggie stomped into my writing room and plopped the newspaper on my computer keyboard, making it impossible for me to continue the inane drivel I was writing at the time.

Aggie put her hands on her hips, raised up to her full height of 4 feet 11 inches, and said, "You know all about this stuff! You're always chasing off bears and lions. Kids are getting hurt out there. You should write a book helping these people out... Now!"

Yes, Dear!

PROLOGUE

Attacked!

Fear threatened to choke the blood from my wildly beating heart, and I fought back the panicked impulse to run. Violent trembling consumed my body, and my breath came in short, ragged gasps.

I blinked my eyes, hoping that the nightmare in front of me might indeed be an apparition that would disappear between blinks. But this was worse than a nightmare. This was deadly reality that stared back at me with the pale yellow eyes of a lethal killer.

I'd first spotted the huge mountain lion 60 yards away paralleling me as I hiked the Forest Service trail in Montana. I'd hoped the lion was just passing in the same direction, but whenever I slowed down, the lion slowed. When I hurried, the lion hurried.

Twice, I lost sight of the lion and was startled to see the big cat cross the trail less than 40 yards in front of me. The longer I walked, the bolder the lion became. Finally, the lion loped out of sight, and I hoped that my nightmare had ended. Instead, it had just begun.

I tentatively approached a bend in the trail, hoping for the best, but expecting the worst. I got the worst. The big cat lay crouched beside a log about 30 feet from the trail, waiting. His ears were laid back, and his tail twitched back and forth.

I'd known that if I traveled through lion country long enough, sooner or later I would find myself in exactly this predicament. I had long ago prepared for such an encounter.

Though I carried no gun, I was not defenseless.

The next move was the lion's. Would he turn and run, like most, or would he charge? He answered with body tensed and legs bunched, ready to spring.

The next move was mine. A loud blast of pepper spray shot forward in a huge orange ball and engulfed the startled cat. It leaped six feet into the air, snarling and pawing at its face. The lion hit the ground and disappeared into the forest in a blur.

Mike Lapinski
August 10, 1998

INTRODUCTION

This Book Could Save Your Life!

A mountain lion kills a ten-year-old Colorado boy. Another lion severely mauls a California woman. A coyote drags a three-year-old boy away from a rural Cape Cod backyard. A wild boar pummels a man in North Carolina, and a grizzly bear kills a hiker in Glacier National Park in Montana.

Every year, innocent people are attacked, maimed and even killed by wild animals while enjoying the outdoors. Sadly, most of these incidents could have been avoided if these folks had a plan and the means to defend themselves.

Why the sudden rise in human/animal confrontations? The answer is simple, yet disturbing. Lion numbers have increased dramatically in recent years. Black bears are emerging in areas where they've been absent for decades, and the mighty grizzly bear has increased to the point where it may soon be removed from the Endangered Species list.

In the meantime, their habitat is shrinking under the bulldozer as countless rural subdivisions and resorts are carved into serene natural settings that have been the historic homes of these wild animals. In addition, more people are taking to the woods to enjoy nature and get back to the simpler pleasures in life. The result is more dogs, kids and adults roaming through woods that were once the exclusive domain of the wild animals. An increase in contact between humans and wild animals is inevitable, but an increase in tragedies is not.

That's why I wrote this book. I've written nine other books on outdoor subjects, but none as important as this one. This book could save your life. It could also save you or your loved ones from the trauma of a wild animal attack, or the excruciating pain and horrible disfigurement common from such attacks, to say nothing of the staggering medical bills.

In writing this book, it is my desire to furnish you with enough information to avoid an attack, but if on the odd chance you are attacked, you'll know how to stop a wild animal in its tracks. Ultimately, you'll feel safe in the great outdoors, and if you feel secure, you'll surely enjoy your communion with nature much more.

I am uniquely qualified to write a book about self defense for nature lovers because I not only love the outdoors, I live it. I've spent most of my 52 years travelling through backcountry and enjoying nature. If you spend that much time in the woods, you're bound to find yourself in various predicaments with wild animals.

I've been charged by bears and mountain lions, treed by furious cow moose and rut crazed bull elk, and I've found myself surrounded by poisonous snakes. And then there was the morning I shook the black widow spider out of my boot. As such, I've spent many years learning about wild animals and how to avoid becoming a victim out there. I've also formulated plans to stop any wild animal from attacking. I'm confident that I can, and have, stopped them in their tracks. These methods work for me, and they can work for you, too!

Fear is the number one enemy of any nature lover. It not only robs you of the enjoyment of the outdoors, but it also clouds your thinking. It's also at the root of many attacks. The first impulse of fear is to run, which triggers an instinctive predatory reaction from a wild animal. A hiker who was recently killed in Glacier National Park tried to run away from the bear that killed him. For that reason, my first chapter deals with the critical issue of fear, specifically primal fear, which all humans possess. If you deal with it, understand it and conquer it, you will have taken a giant step toward being able to defend yourself in the outdoors.

But what happens when an animal does attack? Is there an alternative to curling into a human ball and serving yourself up as lunch. Yes! My chapter on self defense weapons and deterrents is a must-read for any nature lover who wants to protect herself or himself and their loved ones.

The saying goes that the best warrior is the one who understands his adversary. Each chapter that deals with a specific wild animal covers the secret lives of such potentially dangerous predators as bears, lions, large mammals, snakes and spiders. By knowing how, why, when and where these animals live their daily lives, you can better understand them, but more importantly, what triggers an aggressive reaction.

In addition, each chapter explains in detail how to avoid those high risk areas where a possible dangerous confrontation may occur. Also covered is the critical issue of how to stop an aggressive wild animal's attack. Hopefully, it will never happen, but if it does, you'll know how to stop even a charging grizzly bear in its tracks.

Six year old Dante Swallow recovers in the hospital room after he was attacked by a mountain lion. (Photo courtesy Kurt Wilson.)

At the end of each chapter will be a "Quick-Check List" of tips on avoiding and stopping a wild animal attack that you can cut out and carry with you for quick reference whenever you venture into the outdoors.

In addition, I'll cover the animal-borne rabies disease, and explain how to identify a rabid animal and avoid being bit. As a bonus, I've also included a special chapter on living safely in a rural home — the place where most animal conflicts occur.

Ancient scripture reminds us that wisdom is better than strength. Arm yourself with knowledge and understanding of the outdoors and its beautiful animals, and then simply arm yourself. You'll not only do a service for yourself and your loved ones, but you'll also save the animals from needless retaliation.

CHAPTER ONE

Overcoming Your Outdoor Fears

Primal Fear

Arlene Simpson was a street-smart Seattle resident who had lived daily with the very real dangers of the inner city for many years and successfully avoided them. Finally, she moved away from all the drugs and crime of the big city to the peaceful, sparsely populated state of Montana. And then she got scared.

This same woman who had shrewdly maneuvered her life for fifty years through some of the most dangerous inner city neighborhoods, and had deftly thwarted all attempts to be preyed upon by human criminals, found herself in an unnerving predicament. For the first time in her life, she felt threatened.

At first, Arlene rationalized it as jitters from being a stranger in a new state. But within months, local folks had befriended Arlene, her two children and husband, Joe. They attended neighborhood barbecues, and her son and daughter had quickly met wonderful new playmates. Joe was at peace after a stressful career as an accountant, and husband and wife had never gotten along better together. As for Arlene, she developed close friendships with several ladies, and never wanted for a friend-in-need.

Still, the fear continued. At first, it was a nagging uneasiness that puzzled her. But as it grew more irrational she became more concerned that she may be harboring a subconscious dislike for this Utopia.

Eventually, Arlene discovered the source of her fear. She simply dreaded going outside. At first, she laughed at such foolishness, but when Arlene further isolated her emotions, she discovered that she had a hysterical fear of the outdoors. Though no one had seen a bear in the neighborhood for years, her skin crawled whenever she ventured into the backyard. Underbrush scared her, deep forest made her wonder what lurked back there, and shadows never found her nearby.

Such newfound feelings also puzzled her. She'd been on many vacations to campgrounds throughout the West and had always thoroughly enjoyed the serenity of nature. Why this

Primal fear causes an irrational fear of the outdoors. That's why most humans instinctively fear the coming of dark. (Photo courtesy Jack Lacey.)

sudden, irrational fear of walking up the country lane to the mailbox three hundred yards away?

After much discussion, Arlene and I agreed that she had a severe case of primal fear. Primal fear resides within all of us, some more than others. Its origin harkens all the way back to the early days of man when Homo Sapiens was fair game for a variety of deadly predators.

You don't think you have it? Take this simple test. At sundown, enter the woods. Even after a short distance of fifty yards or so, you'll feel that nudging in your spirit, warning that you have no business being in those woods in the dark. For some folks, it is just a twinge of uneasiness. For others, it becomes a hysterical impulse to Run! Run! Run! back to the safety of the cave.

I have spent many years travelling and sleeping out under trees in some of the deepest wilderness in America. I'm an experienced woodsman who knows how to live off the land many miles from civilization. And as you've just read, I'm very capable of defending myself. But when the sun slips behind the mountains, those first gloomy shadows of dusk bring rise to a nagging inner sense of trepidation, followed by the thought that I should not be in the woods when it gets dark.

Okay, so we all possess some degree of primal fear. How can we gain control over it, instead of visa versa? The key to defeating it is understanding it and taking steps to keep it in check. That's where good old human reasoning power becomes invaluable. By rationalizing the fear of real harm out there in the woods with perceived danger, our human psyche can allay most of our primal fear, both consciously and subconsciously.

As for me, I quickly remind myself that I'm now at the top of the food chain. I then make a quick check of all the things that can go wrong or harm me, then mentally cancel them with prepared counter measures. By the time I finish with my "Quick-Check List," I feel confident and capable of handling anything out there, and I also experience a peace that allows me to enjoy the outdoors.

You can begin by analyzing and intelligently rationalizing the danger from the most powerful predator out there — the mighty grizzly bear. I once encountered two tourists in Yellowstone National Park who were literally quaking in their designer hiking boots after they realized that they had to walk for two hundred yards in the dark along a lighted path through the woods to their hotel after an evening wildlife seminar.

They were from Newark, New Jersey. No, they had never seen a grizzly bear, but they "just knew" bears were lurking somewhere out there in the dark. I escorted them back to their hotel and explained that a grizzly bear had not attacked a human in Yellowstone in the past three years, and no bear caused deaths had occurred anywhere in America in the past two years. They were stunned by these revelations. One of the ladies quipped, "It seems like we're always hearing or reading about bears killing people in the national parks."

We spoke at length about the real dangers of nature verses the perceived dangers, and I explained the root of their anxiety — primal fear. Before I left them, they vowed to overcome their anxiety by preparing for adversity, and to begin enjoying this natural paradise. One of the ladies called out to me, "Actually, Newark is a lot more dangerous!" The other added with a laugh, "Yeh, there's lots more predators of the two-legged kind back there!"

Now let's examine the possibility of being killed by a bear while on vacation in one of our national parks. After more than 120 years and two hundred million visitors, less than two hundred people have died in all our national parks from all causes, mostly accidents. But only sixteen people have been killed by bears in our national parks — in 120 years!

Here's another good overall eye catcher. In 1997, less than sixty people died from animal, spider and snake bites. In that same time period, auto accidents alone killed almost 50,000 men, women and children! We hurtle down a busy freeway bumper-to-bumper at 85 miles per hour with a yawn, yet we're scared to walk into the woods? That, folks, is instinctive, irrational fear —

primal fear.

After you've satisfied yourself that a menacing wild animal is not hiding behind every bush waiting to pounce on you, the next step in gaining a healthy attitude toward the outdoors is to have a well-rounded understanding of the natural world and the role that these animals play in it. This new understanding further reduces the wild beast from the bloodthirsty killer to an innocent animal.

Understanding Wild Animals

All wild creatures are integral parts of the cycle of nature, where every living organism from the tiny ant up to the huge grizzly bear perform a specific function. And unlike man, who alone has the ability to think and reason, wild animals simply react to stimuli. Where humans harbor evil thoughts and connive to steal, hurt and murder, a wild animal possesses none of these less-than-admirable human traits. Animals are not capable of thinking or reasoning, only reacting. They posses just three simple drives — to eat, mate and survive.

Unfortunately, much of the irrational fear of wild animals is derived from inaccurate portrayals of wild animals in books and movies, where they suddenly possess demonic, craving intentions. In the movies, wolves run in huge packs and tear humans to pieces, even though there has not been one recorded human death from a wolf in the history of America. Other movies show poisonous spiders or snakes lying in wait to pounce on human victims, while the truth of the matter is that every snake or spider that I've ever encountered retreated immediately. And speaking of Gentle Ben, when was the last time a bear acted biologically accurate in a movie? The list of inaccuracies goes on and on, and has served the unfortunate purpose of injecting unnatural fear into the human mind to consider every wild animal a cunning killer.

I've been close to hundreds of the most powerful predators in the wilds, ranging from bears to lions, and most wanted nothing more than to vacate the area after becoming aware of my presence. Instead of being four-legged demons, wild animals are innocent creatures who perform a function to keep nature simple and beautiful. The lion hunts and kills deer because the deer population must be kept in check or massive starvation will result. The average snake will have swallowed hundreds of rats and mice in its lifetime, thereby ridding croplands and homes of these pests. Spiders just want to eat bugs, and bears just want to fill their bellies and lay around.

The critical point to understand here is that every wild animal is not out to bite, sting, claw or maul every human it encounters. It just wants to eat, sleep, mate and survive. However, when a wild animal is starving, disturbed, or threatened, that animal may react aggressively to counteract these disturbances to its natural routine. And therein lies the scenario for a confrontation between human and animal.

You may have all the best intentions in the world, and in fact love the mother black bear that suddenly threatens you with bodily harm after you accidentally stumbled upon its cubs. You are innocent, and the mother bear is innocent. You just want to get out of there without getting attacked, and the bear just wants to protect her babies.

Yet all this noble prose about innocence becomes wasted rhetoric when a bear is coming at you. It is your right, even your responsibility, to defend yourself. But how? It's too late to postulate on how you could have avoided this confrontation. You need to stop that onrushing bear NOW!

That's why you need to formulate a plan of self defense in your mind long before you take to the outdoors. Obviously, preparation is the key to surviving a confrontation with a wild animal, but what defense can a human have against a huge charging grizzly bear, or a stalking mountain lion, or a furious cow moose? The good news is that there are deterrents that can stop even the most determined attack by any of the largest, most dangerous mammals in America.

What about Arlene Simpson? She now enjoys her country life. She studied the habits of bears and learned when and where they are most likely to be on the move. She also knows how to avoid them and how to stop them. She's not afraid of bears anymore, but she still is wary. And that's ok. That's normal. She now carries a defense against bears with her most, but not all, of the time when she is outdoors. After all, she has a right to defend herself.

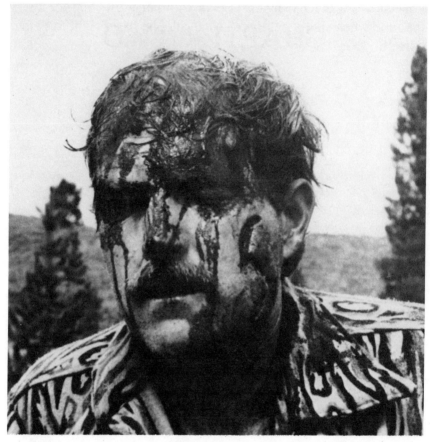

Mark Matheny was mauled by a grizzly bear when he stumbled upon the bear's food cache. Mark now carries pepper spray for self defense. (Photo courtesy Mark Matheny.)

CHAPTER TWO

Choosing A Defensive Weapon

There are two main methods used to stop an attacking animal. The first is deadly force, and the second is a deterrent. Both are capable of protecting a person. However, a wide gulf exists between the consequences of the two, ranging from the overall definition of self defense to the danger posed by the weapon itself to the operator and the people she or he may be entrusted to protect.

Specifically, use of deadly force translates to a gun, while a deterrent means pepper spray. In my opinion, there is no right or wrong choice here because every human life is sacred. No matter what extenuating circumstances or noble purpose are behind a wild animal's attack, no one deserves to be subjected to injury, maiming or death from claw or fang. Every human being has the right to defend themselves by any means necessary to stop an attack.

However, much thought should be given to your choice of a weapon because there are legal, ethical and moral issues involved. It's not a decision to be taken lightly, and as you will read, each choice carries its own unique consequences.

Deadly Force

The purpose of a firearm is to kill whatever you shoot at. A bullet traveling at 2,000 feet per second will tear a gaping hole through any flesh it strikes. If death is not the immediate result, a slow death usually results later from shock, blood loss or infection.

If your choice of defensive weapon is a gun, you should

understand that you'll probably kill any advancing animal you hit. A certain faction would reply, "Who cares, when a mean old bear is trying to kill me!" I totally agree with that sentiment.

However, it becomes more complicated when it's not a mean old boar grizzly that comes storming out of the brush at you. It may be a sow black bear defending her cubs, and you're not totally sure if she intends to attack you, or just bluff you. Pull the trigger, and you've just created two orphan cubs who will almost certainly die if left to fend for themselves in the wild. Still, the fact remains that a bullet in the vitals of an attacking animal is the best way to kill it.

Montana resident Doug Thielmann lives in grizzly bear country and wanted to be sure that if he was ever attacked by a large animal, he would be able to stop it. Period! For self defense, he chose one of the most powerful handguns in the world, a Smith & Wesson .44 magnum revolver.

Doug's brother, Scott, is an experienced woodsman and warned Doug, "Most people couldn't hit a grizzly standing broadside, let alone charging. If you intend to carry that gun, make sure you can hit something with it."

That was sage advice because two months later while bowhunting, Doug hiked around a bend in a Forest Service trail in the Gallatin National Forest north of Yellowstone and encountered a sow grizzly with two half grown cubs. As Doug slowly backed away, the sow false charged twice before stopping each time about thirty yards away.

Finally, the bear laid back her ears and charged forward, fast and low. Doug knew that this time she would not stop. When the sow was only ten feet away, Doug shot her between the eyes and killed her in mid-stride. The U.S. Fish and Wildlife Service investigated the incident and quickly labeled it a legal self-defense killing, totally exonerating Doug.

However, several people have mentioned to Doug that the sow's life could have been spared if he'd used pepper spray. It would be an understatement to say that it rankles him. He told me, "Those people weren't there. It's easy for them to say 'save the bear', but if they had lived through what I went through, I'd be willing to bet they'd have been happy to have that .44 magnum in their hand. That sow meant to kill me, and I believe I possibly saved other human lives by killing her because I found out later that she was a problem bear."

Doug added, "As for those 'poor' cubs, they were yearlings that already weighed over two hundred pounds. In fact, they came back the next day and ate the dead sow. In two days, there wasn't hardly any sign of that sow left except some hide and hair."

The grizzly that Doug Thielmann killed with a .44 magnum pistol after it had charged him. U.S. Fish & Wildlife agents removed the bear's head and claws to prevent illegal trafficking in bear parts. (Photo courtesy Doug Thielmann.)

In my opinion, the greatest drawback to using a pistol for self defense lies in the fact that it is a very short range weapon. A pistol's short barrel and sighting system allow accurate shots out to only about forty yards even under controlled firing range conditions for the average shooter. However, most shooters don't become even that proficient with a high powered handgun because of the unpleasant recoil, rendering the average pistol efficient only at point blank range.

There is another very real ingredient to this escalating pistol problem — shock. It's very traumatic to be charged by a bear or lion. I should know; I've been charged by both! Your mind scrambles just to stay functional during those few adrenalin charged seconds before the animal is on you. Few of us have the calmness to draw our pistol, carefully aim, and squeeze off an accurate shot, as Doug Thielmann did.

Suggested Calibers

The caliber of handgun you choose should depend upon the region where you live. A 9mm automatic, or .38 Special caliber would be appropriate for self defense in southern states where danger comes more in the form of snakes, or wild boars and feral dogs. Along the East Coast, where black bears roam, .45 caliber or .357 magnum caliber are advisable to stop these bigger animals.

In the West where black bears, grizzly bears and mountain lions roam, a .357 magnum or .44 magnum caliber is advisable, and most opt for the more powerful .44 magnum. But be forewarned, you still have to be able to hit what you're aiming at to be effective, and these magnum calibers deliver a punishing wallop on both ends of the barrel. The .44 magnum especially delivers a tremendous knuckle-bleeding kick, plus a concussion that tends to leave you shell shocked after a half dozen shots.

Legal Problems With Firearms

Many states now make it virtually impossible to legally own a handgun. And even if your state allows you to own one, you will probably break several laws while travelling through these states with a pistol during your vacation. There are many horror stories of innocent travelers being detained, even arrested, for interstate transportation of a concealed, unregistered handgun.

In addition, it is illegal to possess a firearm in any national park. Every year vacationers find themselves in trouble with park rangers for carrying or defending themselves with a handgun that was illegal to possess within the park boundary.

The Dangers of Firearms

I recently viewed an old African Safari video which showed a hunter being attacked by a leopard. The animal sprang from out of nowhere onto the hunter and ferociously clawed and bit the man. The guide quickly ran up to the leopard, wedged his firearm against the big cat's chest and squeezed the trigger. The

A high caliber pistol is one choice for a self defense weapon. However, this choice should be given serious thought because of moral, ethical and legal issues.

tremendous impact of the high powered rifle blew the cat backwards about six feet, and it was dead when it hit the ground.

That was the good news. The bad news was that the hunter's hand was also blown six feet away with the leopard. The hunter was attempting to push the cat away and had his hand directly in front of the barrel when the gun was fired.

The stories get worse, and more tragic. A few years ago, a man was attacked by a black bear. The man's son ran up and shot the black bear. The bullet killed the bear instantly, but continued through the bear and also killed the young man's father.

In addition, it is a sad fact that self defense handguns are one of the leading causes of accidental deaths among children in America. Because of video games and movies glorifying guns, kids are attracted to handguns like bees to honey. If you choose to use a handgun for self defense outdoors, never leave it unattended in your vehicle or in camp. At home, always use a trigger guard that the kids can't figure out. It is this very real danger, far greater than any bear, that causes many outdoors people to seek an alternative self defense weapon.

Pepper Spray Deterrents

In recent years deterrent sprays have appeared on the market to stop an aggressive animal without killing it. The main ingredient in these sprays is Oleoresin Capsicum, the active ingredient in hot red peppers. This extremely volatile substance immediately turns all moist membrane red hot, including the eyes, mouth, lungs, nose and lips.

An animal that receives a shot of pepper spray in the face will be temporarily blinded and feel immediate intense pain in the eyes and mouth. It will have difficulty breathing. No matter what intentions an aggressive wild animal may have had during its charge, it will quickly revert to a survival mode and flee.

I once allowed myself to be exposed to a small dose of this pepper spray, just to see how it would affect a wild animal. Boy, that was quite an education! My mouth and lips burned like fire, and my eyes hurt so bad that I could barely see for about ten minutes. But remember, I exposed myself to only a very small amount of pepper spray.

There is also an exciting report that a new active ingredient now being studied may make pepper spray even more effective. Currently, the habanero pepper is being tested as a further improvement in pepper spray potency. The habanero is 60 times hotter than its fiery cousin, the jalapeno, and 10 times hotter than the cayenne used in today's pepper spray. Hopefully, all the legal obstacles will soon be hurdled to get this exciting new pepper into cans for self defense use outdoors.

Countless Pepper Spray Testimonies

Mark Matheny is one of the leading authorities on pepper spray. After being attacked and horribly mauled by a grizzly bear, Mark spent a few years armed to the teeth whenever he ventured into the woods. But Mark had a problem with that. He loved the wilds and the bears that lived there. He especially admired the grizzly bear, yet he found himself making elaborate plans to shoot the next one that came near him.

Mark eventually created UDAP (Universal Defense Alternative Products) Pepper Spray. It is one of the hottest, most dependable pepper sprays on the market today. From his Bozeman, Montana, home, Mark told me, "You can't believe the number of pepper spray testimonials I receive every year. Guys are stopping charging grizzly bears in their tracks with pepper spray. Hikers are spraying lions and saving kids. I even got a testimonial about a guy who uses my pepper spray back East against wild boars."

Mark continued, "The nice thing about all these testimonials is that in every incident the aggressive animal was never killed, but it did receive a hot dose of adverse conditioning."

Mark's comment about adverse conditioning was echoed by a warden who removes problem bears from U.S. Air Force stations in Alaska. He told me, "I've sprayed more than 2,000 bears, some of them charging me. Every one immediately left the area and didn't come back. I hate to shoot a bear, and this pepper spray does a great job of associating human habitations with an unpleasant experience for the bears."

How To Use Pepper Spray

Pepper spray is under tremendous pressure in the can. Unlike your home bug spray that hisses out of the can in a small aerosol mist, pepper spray is very loud and blasts out of the can in a huge orange oil based cloud. In fact, the noise resembles a .22 rifle shot which in itself has the potential to startle and stop an aggressive animal.

In a micro-second a huge airborne red ball shoots thirty feet out and fifteen feet wide. The oil base keeps the orange cloud suspended for several seconds, so you don't have to be accurate or wait until the animal is literally on top of you. Usually, a charging animal is sprayed when it is still twenty yards away (60 feet). The fast charging attacker will run into the orange cloud and stop in painful bewilderment, choking and pawing at its face. In the

Pepper spray has proven effective in stopping most bear attacks. It is a non-lethal alternative to a firearm.

meantime, you should slowly back away. If necessary, put another blast of pepper spray between you and the predator.

Pepper Spray Is Safe

A kid playing with a pistol is a tragedy waiting to happen. A kid playing with a can of pepper spray is a very painful lesson waiting to be learned, but no injury will result, although the kid may think he's going to die for the first few minutes. That's because pepper spray is nothing more than hot red pepper dust and causes no permanent injury or damage, with most of its effects gone within a half hour.

In the past few years, more stories have emerged about outdoors people stopping attacks with pepper spray than with guns. During that time, no people have died from an accidental shot of pepper spray, a claim that cannot be made from the handgun camp.

Pepper Spray Is Not A Repellent!

Recently, pepper spray has received some negative newspaper coverage because a single person in Alaska observed bears sniffing and rolling in red pepper spray that had been applied to personal items as a repellent to discourage bears from chewing on them. Some parents have even sprayed their children!

Inert red pepper and oil actually is attractive to a bear, but that is not the purpose of pepper spray. It's designed to be a deterrent, not a repellent! Mark Matheny shakes his head at this misuse of pepper spray. "It's designed to be sprayed into the face of an oncoming predator," he emphasizes. "It's not bug spray!"

Conclusion

I've used both firearms and pepper spray for self defense outdoors. I've decided to go with the pepper spray because it is safe for me and everyone else with me. I also truly love all the wild animals out there, most of whom are simply reacting out of fear. I don't want to be killed by one of them, but I don't want to kill them, either. Pepper spray accomplishes all the above.

You, too, must choose which form of self defense is best. But remember, there is no gun or pepper spray that is 100% effective in stopping every charging wild animal. It is a sobering fact that there have been instances when a gun or pepper spray has failed to stop an attack. For that reason, it's best to take steps beforehand to avoid a potentially dangerous confrontation. The best way to accomplish that is to understand where the potentially dangerous wild animals live in your area, where they are most likely to be found, and then plan to avoid those areas.

CHAPTER THREE

The Mountain Lion

Status

Mountain lion numbers have increased dramatically throughout the western states, due mainly to a marked increase in deer, their natural prey. However, deer numbers have dwindled in recent years because of severe winters. The result is a large lion population and not enough natural prey to hunt.

In addition, many housing developments, including vacation and ski resorts, continue to creep into historical lion habitat, leading to the inevitable confrontation between humans and lions. Just north of where I live in Montana, several lions have invaded rural subdivisions and killed livestock and dogs in recent months, a sure sign that a lion (or should we say human) overpopulation exists. If you live in a rural home in lion country, take special precautions, as detailed below, to protect pets and children.

Another perplexing situation that has contributed to the lion overpopulation is the unwarranted over-protection of lions. Erroneous information was circulated several years ago that the big cats were in danger of extinction, and several movie stars publicly appealed for the protection of the lion. It was unfounded numerically, and unsound biologically, yet several states severely restricted lion hunting, and some even banned it.

For instance, California banned lion hunting, against overwhelming opposition by state wildlife biologists. Lion problems increased dramatically. People were harassed, attacked and even killed by lions. In fact, there are more lions killed on

Report any lion sightings near your home to authorities.

California highways right now than were allowed to be killed by hunting.

Lion Behavior

The mountain lion is a natural born killer. It eats neither grass nor berries. It kills and eats large animals to survive. Deer comprise about 95 percent of a lion's diet, but this big cat is fully capable of bringing down much larger animals, such as elk and moose.

A mature male lion weighs about 190 pounds, while a female weighs about 140 pounds. Its color is tan, and it has a smallish head, short legs and a long body with a four foot long tail.

You can gauge the stealth and power of this big predator by studying the animals it hunts. Experienced hunters will tell you that the whitetail deer's senses of detection are extremely keen, making it difficult to kill one even with a long range rifle, yet a lion is able to sneak up and catch a deer with its claws. Gulp! On the other hand, the powerful bull elk weighs a half ton and carries a wicked rack of antlers, yet the lion is fully capable of breaking its neck. Thank God most lions are instinctively fearful of humans!

Few lions are spotted by humans because they are very secretive and prefer to travel in dense brush or forest. They usually skirt openings and seek deep shadows to lessen the chance of their prey spotting them. Most deer live in brushy areas where they find feed plentiful, and that is where the lion is normally found.

When a lion spots a deer, it quickly assesses the terrain ahead and checks the wind direction. It then moves forward rapidly until it is within a hundred yards of its prey. The lion then begins stalking forward. Its short legs allow the lion to hug the ground, and a one-foot diameter log is enough to shield it from the sharp-eyed deer.

When the deer's head is down, the lion flits between logs and bushes as it moves forward. When the deer picks its head up, the lion freezes in mid-stride until the deer returns to feeding. When the lion stalks to within thirty yards of the deer, it bunches its legs and prepares to charge.

The next time the deer drops its head, the lion leaps forward and is usually on the startled deer before it has a chance to escape. Normally, the lion bites the deer's neck and kills it quickly. A lion does not like to eat putrid meat, so in summer it will feed on a deer for only a few days before moving on, but in winter it may gnaw on a deer carcass for a week or more.

HOW TO AVOID A LION
Avoid Dense Cover And Make Noise

A lion's existence depends on being silent and stealthy. That's the secret to a lion's hunting success. It's also the key to avoiding a lion because the big cat does not like to be discovered. Unlike bears, which tend to be aggressive and confrontational when startled, a surprised lion is usually unnerved when exposed and flees into cover where it feels secure.

The best way to avoid a lion is to avoid heavy cover, especially where numerous deer live. If I'm in an area where I've seen lion tracks, or discovered a lion kill, I'll stay clear of brushy areas where the natural hunting instincts in a lion may be aroused. By staying at least fifty yards in the open, you will force any aggressive lion to stalk into the open and expose itself, something most cats hate to do.

If you must walk through a brushy area, make lots of noise. I usually bark like a dog. Lions hate the racket of barking dogs. Any lion could quickly kill two baying hunting hounds, but it instead climbs a tree just to escape the racket! Simulate baying hounds, and you usually won't see any lion that may have been lurking in the brush ahead — because they hate the noise!

Lions And Food

Unlike a grizzly bear, a lion is not dangerously aggressive protecting its food, and it's usually a simple chore to avoid a lion on its food cache. When a lion makes a kill, it drags its prey close to cover and then scrapes leaves and twigs over the carcass to hide it from birds or other predators. This is a very conspicuous heaped pile of freshly disturbed forest debris, and often shows deer legs or antlers sticking out of it.

If you spot one of these kill sites, do not investigate it because the lion will be resting nearby. Even if you do walk onto a kill site and encounter the lion, you're still fairly safe because with a full belly the lion is not in a predatory mode, but is merely protecting its food. Slowly retreat, and the lion will normally leave you alone.

Remove Undergrowth Near Dwellings

Many lion confrontations occur close to rural homesites where dense brush grows at the edge of the property. Many dogs and children have been attacked by lions that suddenly sprang from underbrush that was allowed to grow within charging distance of

A lion uses trees and rocks to hide behind and normally avoids open terrain while hunting. If you hike in open terrain, you'll greatly reduce the chances of a sudden close range lion encounter.

the back yard, usually about thirty yards.

A few years back, a young lion sprang from a tangle of brush growing at the edge of a backyard of a rural home in western Montana and attacked a five-year-old boy. The lion killed the child and dragged the body into the brush, where it was partially consumed. Authorities brought in a lion hunter with dogs, who quickly treed and killed the lion.

If you live in lion country, it is imperative to cut down the brush near your home and force the lion to move through the area farther back where dense cover hides its movement, and it is not within the proximity of humans or pets and is thereby less tempted to turn predatory.

It's also a good idea to erect a woven wire fence around the children's play area. A determined lion can still get over a fence, but it will have to expose itself, and lions don't like to lose the element of surprise. Besides, a lion climbing over a fence is sure to alert the kids and they'll have time to flee into the house.

Be Alert To Lion Activity In Your Area

The sad epilogue to the above tragedy is that the presence of a lion in that neighborhood was known. Two dogs had been killed and eaten by a lion in the weeks before the child was attacked, and a lion had been spotted by residents. If you see a lion near a home, or hear of dogs being attacked, call the local wildlife office and demand that lion hunting dogs be brought out to chase away any lions in the vicinity.

Don't Allow Salt Blocks Near Your Home

This one should be a no-brainer. Unfortunately, well-meaning, but biologically ignorant, nature lovers who move into rural areas love to watch deer outside the back window. And since deer crave salt in spring and summer, a salt block is often placed near the home so the inhabitants can look at all the cute deer frolicking nearby.

This concentrates the deer, and the lions move in. I don't have enough fingers and toes to count the times I've heard about lions literally moving into rural subdivisions and roaming between homes hunting deer. The deer are not stupid. With a lion nearby, they vacate the area. Strange things then begin to happen in the neighborhood. House cats disappear; then dogs. So what's left for a starving lion to eat when the dogs and cats are gone? The answer should be obvious.

I had an experience that chillingly illustrates the problem of deer concentrated near rural homes. I received a call from a man who had recently moved to Montana. The man had built a beautiful home nestled in the pines. He also created a lovely garden, orchard and lawn, and he'd placed a salt block 60 yards from the house so the family could watch the deer from the kitchen window. Of course, all these enticements drew the deer in like a magnet and created havoc with his landscaping.

The man asked me to remove a few of the deer, so I set up a treestand forty yards behind his garage and planned to harvest three does with a bow and arrow. The first morning, I was in the treestand, but the deer seemed jumpy. I soon discovered why. A large lion sneaked around a corner of the garage and walked right under a treehouse that the guy's two kids had erected that summer!

I called an experienced lion hunter, who came over and quickly treed and harvested that lion. I'll never forget the sight of that lion padding silently beneath those kids' treehouse.

Shield Children From Young Lions

Two recent lion attacks are typical of the dangers presented to small people in lion country. In Colorado's Rocky Mountain National Park, an exuberant youngster scrambled ahead and out of sight of his family on a trail. The family was horrified to find the dead boy being dragged off by a mountain lion. In Montana, a large group of six year olds were on a summer camp outing, led by three teenagers. A lion stalked up behind the group and grabbed the last kid. Fortunately, a counselor was able to beat back the lion and save the boy.

These incidents illustrate two very critical lion behavioral traits that can help people avoid an attack. One of the biggest discoveries from the recent upsurge in lion attacks is that children have been the targets. The other discovery was that most of the problem lions have been young animals kicked out of their home range by larger dominant lions.

These yearling cats, averaging about 90-120 pounds, were chased away from their mother when it was time for her to have another litter of kittens. The dominant mature lions in the area jealously guard their hunting territory, and they'll kill a young lion if it does not vacate the area. These lions eventually are forced into new lands, where they don't know the best hunting areas, and after a while they become emaciated, starved and desperate. This is the scenario of just about every lion attack in recent years.

The obvious answer to avoiding an attack in lion country is to keep youngsters close to adults. Two recent incidents illustrate the effectiveness of this simple preventive measure. Twice in western Montana, families out for an evening walk discovered young lions stalking them. The adults shielded the small children and cautiously retreated. The aggressive young lions stalked within ten feet of the adults, but lacked the confidence to initiate an attack against such a large adversary, given the bad experiences they surely must have had when chased off by bigger cats. Also, these folks were hiking in open terrain and spotted the lions, thereby thwarting the lion's element of a surprise attack and subjecting the secretive cat to the pressure of discovery and scrutiny.

But remember to always put an adult in front and behind. Despite the heroics of the teenager to save the young summer camp boy from the clutches of the lion, this attack might have been prevented if one of the camp counselors had dropped back and shielded the kids from a rear attack by the young lion.

HOW TO STOP A LION ATTACK!
Do Not Run Away!

Any lion that advances toward a human is already in a predatory mode, but the cat may be unsure about a person being easy prey. But if you turn and run, you will surely trigger a predatory reaction in that lion. Never run away from a lion!

A mountain lion relies on stealth and cover to hunt. Lions are rarely seen in the West because they seek the seclusion of undergrowth.

Instead, stand your ground and try to look big. Slowly back away, always facing the lion.

Sticks And Stones May Scare Away A Lion

Unlike the bear, which may react aggressively to a hefty rock thrown at it, a lion is easily startled by thrown objects and the noises they make. Sticks or rocks thrown at a lion are aggressive actions that may confuse an advancing lion and thwart an attack.

I once encountered a huge male lion only 20 yards away along a brushy trail in Montana. Rather than run away, the lion slowly circled me in the brush. I had pepper spray, so my life was not in danger. I then did a little impromptu experimenting. I picked up a large rock and threw it at the lion. The poorly thrown rock landed two feet behind the lion.

However, the rock noisily crashing through the brush made that lion jump four feet straight into the air, and it spun around in mid-air to face the spot where the rock had crashed. In an instant, the lion was gone. The combination of noise, plus the unsettling notion that "something unknown" was behind it, totally unnerved that big lion.

Barking Works!

Here's a good experiment for you to do in the safety of your home. Sit your dog down and then have everyone start making loud barking sounds. The dog will become excited and join in the fun. Now sit your cat down and begin barking loudly. Zip! No more cat!

If you spot a lion close by, start making very loud and aggressive barking sounds. The louder and more intense, the better. If you don't have a loud voice, buy an aerosol noise maker

The two year old lion that attacked Dante Swallow weighed only about 110 pounds and is typical of the occasional immature lion that may become desperate enough to pursue smaller prey such as children. (Photo courtesy Kurt Wilson.)

that emits an extremely loud shrieking noise. The fact remains that loud, aggressive noise has driven off more lions than any other method.

Make Yourself Big — And Dangerous!

Lions are easily intimidated by other large, aggressive animals. If a lion approaches, raise yourself up to look as large as possible. Spread out your arms and let that lion know that you are big and tough. Yell, wave a stick, throw rocks, bark, growl — do anything and everything to bluff that cat into thinking it would be a big mistake to tangle with you.

Firearms

The most effective method of stopping a lion attack is a gun. Any lion that is advancing on a human poses a threat to that person, and any other people in the area. It is not only a sure way to stop an attack, but it should also be the responsibility of that person to make sure the lion doesn't slink off and find some kid off by himself.

Strangely, warning shots fired nearby don't always stop an aggressive lion. I once had a lion shadow me along a forest trail, and I fired several shots — first, over its head, but when that didn't work I shot twice and kicked up the dirt in front of the lion. Fortunately, I was close to my pickup during this incident. I did not kill this lion because it was not actually attacking me, or showing aggressive behavior.

Pepper Spray

I firmly believe that every traveler in lion country should carry pepper spray — even the kids! I furnished my seven year old grandson, Tommy, with a can of UDAP pepper spray. He's been instructed on how to use it, and how it will really hurt him if he gets to playing with it and accidentally sprays himself.

There have been a few incidents when pepper spray was not 100% effective with bears, but I've never heard of a lion receiving a blast of the hot pepper and continuing forward. The one aggressive lion that I hit with pepper spray disappeared in a blur! The combination of noise, and the instant orange ball with its fiery effects are just too much for the nervous feline.

And if a lion should attack and have a person down in your hiking group, get over there quickly and spray that lion before it inflicts any more damage to its victim. At this stage, a little hot pepper that hits a person in the jaws of a lion is the least of their problems.

Stay Alert!

The one constant in thwarting any lion attack is to see that lion before it gets within charging range. While you are communing with nature — looking at the birds and watching the dainty deer — STAY ALERT! Scan ahead to nearby logs, shadows and brush patches for anything unusual. Remember, with wild animals wisdom is better than strength.

MOUNTAIN LION QUICK-CHECK LIST

To Avoid A Lion At Home
1. Remove undergrowth close to dwellings.
2. Fence in the area of the yard where children will be playing. Use a woven wire livestock fence. A lion can still climb over the fence, but it will be forced to expose itself.
3. Don't use salt blocks to attract deer. Deer attract lions.
4. Report suspicious lion-related activity, such as missing pets.
5. Report any lion sighting and insist lion hounds chase it away.
6. Educate your children about lion behavior.

To Avoid A Lion Outdoors
1. Hike in a group of at least four.
2. Place adults in front of, and behind, children.
3. Don't allow children to move away from adults while hiking.
4. Avoid areas of dense cover.
5. Avoid areas where deer congregate.
6. Make lots of noise.

7. Do not run away from a lion!

To Stop A Lion Attack

1. Stand upright and spread out your arms to appear large.
2. Make lots of noise; bark like a dog.
3. Slowly retreat without turning your back on the lion.
4. If unarmed, throw rocks or sticks at the lion.
5. If unarmed, fight any attack with feet, fists, hiking stick, fishing pole, but stay on your feet.
6. If armed with a gun, fire a few warning shots over the lion's head or in the dirt in front of it.
7. If armed with pepper spray, shoot when the lion stalks to within 30 feet. Start shooting at 60 feet if the lion is running toward you.
8. If armed, consider any lion within 20 yards to be a threat to your safety.

Most black bears quickly leave the area when they become aware of man's presence.

CHAPTER FOUR

The Black Bear

Status
Problems occur with the black bear when people fail to respect and treat it as a potentially dangerous predator. While the grizzly bear has a well deserved reputation for being potentially dangerous, a black bear is often taken lightly. Folks in Yellowstone National Park who run for the safety of their vehicles when a grizzly is sighted, will walk boldly toward a feeding black bear. Big mistake! Black bears annually cause far more damage and injuries to humans than grizzlies.

This is due to the fact that there are many times more black bears in America than grizzlies. In addition, black bears are rapidly expanding their range throughout America. Several midwestern and southern states which had long ago lost their bear populations, now have black bears. They also now have black bear problems because, unlike the solitary grizzly, the black bear is not adverse to living close to human populations. Black bears and humans — often a deadly mix for both sides.

Though not nearly as aggressive as the surly grizzly, black bears are still bruins, and they react aggressively to certain conditions. The best way to avoid becoming a statistic with a black bear is to learn what triggers an aggressive response.

Black Bear Behavior
Black bears are omnivorous, meaning they eat both plants and flesh. A black bear will eat just about anything, though 90 percent of its diet consists of grass, plants, nuts and berries. But above all else, a black bear is a glutton. It will readily seek out high protein

food sources such as a beehive, a can full of putrid garbage, or a rotting animal carcass. It is also not adverse to creating its own carrion if an opportunity to pounce on a deer or young elk arises.

Bears are also very powerful animals. A 150 pound black bear can tear apart a log in a matter of minutes, and a hungry bear can easily tear the siding off a camper trailer. I once observed a black bear crushing cans of food with a single bite of its powerful jaws. And forget that notion about a smallish black bear being safe. The quip among bear experts is that the only difference between a 150 and a 300 pound black bear, is that the smaller bear takes smaller bites.

In early spring, the black bears are gaunt and ravenous fresh out of hibernation. They seek anything to fill their bellies, which usually sends them to grassy areas where they gobble up succulent young grass shoots and other plants such as dandelions and wild parsnips. This often results in an inaccurate portrayal of the black bear as a benign grass eater. That same bear that is observed amiably nipping dandelion buds in May becomes a deadly predator in June when deer, elk and moose drop their young.

Black bears roam these birthing areas and exact a horrible toll of newborn mammals. In some areas of the West, wildlife managers have allowed extra hunting tags to cut down on black bear predation among big game herds. Anyone who believes the black bear is nothing more than a big black dog should view one of these powerful predators running down a calf elk and then chasing off the frantic mother.

How to Avoid Black Bears

The key to avoiding black bears is to learn the four situations that provoke aggressive bear behavior. They are: a startled bear, a hungry bear, a bear defending its food, and a predatory bear. If you can avoid getting into these conflicts with a bear, you should never have a bear problem.

A Startled Black Bear

A bear's reaction to a sudden confrontation with a human is

The black bear is responsible for more property damage and human injuries than the grizzly bear because the black bear is far more numerous and tends to live closer to civilization.

much different from a lion's. The secretive lion's first impulse upon being startled is to flee. A black bear's first impulse may be to confront its adversary. I've run smack into black bears many times on trails. Most ran away like scared rabbits, but four bears woofed, snapped their teeth and made false charges. I ended up blasting one of these bears with pepper spray after it had advanced to within forty feet. But in retrospect, none of the animals had flat out charged me. I had not given them ample warning to flee, and they simply felt threatened by my sudden appearance.

Most close range bear encounters occur in brush where sight distance may be reduced to fifty yards or less. If you want to avoid a bear, avoid hiking through brushy areas. That's not always possible, so the next best thing is to make enough noise that the bear becomes aware of your arrival and has time to retreat without feeling threatened.

Many hikers wear large bear bells fastened to their backpacks.

These bells are better than nothing, but their tinkle usually doesn't carry well through the brush, or is drowned out by a rushing stream where most brush grows.

The best way to alert a bear to your presence is to make a lot of noise, singing and clapping your hands, as you move into dense cover. I once watched a large black bear meandering down a brushy trail three hundred yards away. Presently, two hikers rounded a bend in the trail two hundred yards from the bear and began singing and yelling as they entered the brushy area. The bear heard the commotion, stood on its hind legs for a few seconds, and then barreled down off the trail. Those two hikers probably hoped no one had heard their silly antics. Thank goodness the bear did!

As stupid as this may sound, some people get into trouble with a sow black bear and cubs when they stay put while the bears walk close to them. They are under the false impression that a sow with cubs will somehow understand that they mean her cubs no harm, and they find out too late that any human within 50 yards of her babies is considered a threat. Also, bears don't have great eyesight, and many hikers who stand in the open make the mistake of thinking that the sow has seen them and has accepted them as harmless. Too late, the sow suddenly spots them and becomes aggressive. If you see a sow with cubs, back off and circle them, or find a different trail to hike that day.

Also, bears tend to lose their nerve when outnumbered. For that reason, hikers often travel in groups. Four hikers are usually enough to put any black bear to flight.

A Hungry Black Bear

Bears are attracted to food, period! If you want to avoid having a bear look you up, keep your camp and yourself free of food and food odors. This is really a simple chore and will reduce the chances of a bear confrontation by about 90 percent. There really is no reason for most black bears to bother campers if no food is present.

But if you fail to keep your camp free of food, you're

begging for trouble, like the couple in Montana who had stored snacks inside their tent before taking a hike. When they returned, a sow and her cub were inside the tent eating the snacks. The man hurried to the tent and hollered to chase the bears away. The sow felt threatened and charged, knocking the man down and biting his shoulder and scalp. The bear then knocked the woman down and bit her several times before running off with its cub. This was a classic case of doubling your trouble. The campers had not only left food in camp, but had also startled the sow and allowed no room for her to retreat.

At camp, stow your food inside a bag and hang it by a rope about eighteen feet up a tree, but away from the trunk. Otherwise, a bear will climb the tree and still be able to get at the food. This bag should be kept at least a hundred yards from camp. In addition, set up a second small site to do your cooking about a hundred yards from your main camp. That way, there will be no attractive cooking odors at the site where you'll be sleeping.

Most experienced campers in bear country carry freeze dried food because it has a minimum of odor. Also, if you intend to catch fish and eat them, clean them in the stream far from where you camp, and make sure you bring no tantalizing fish odor back to your main camp on your clothing.

A Black Bear Defending Its Food

Life is harsh for the black bear. It never seems to have enough food and is often forced to eat grass to fill its belly. But instinct drives it in a never-ending quest to build up an ample fat reserve for the long winter months of hibernation ahead. Consequently, a black bear that finds a large source of high protein food, such as a dead animal carcass, sometimes acts aggressive when disturbed.

The best way to avoid a confrontation with a black bear on a carcass is to ask if anyone has seen a bear feeding on carrion in the area you plan to hike. In addition, a bear on a carcass will do a lot of pacing in the area. If you suddenly come across a multitude of black bear tracks, there is a good possibility that a

In late spring, the grass eating black bear often becomes predatory and roams big game birthing areas for newborn.

bear may be nearby guarding its food.

If you stumble upon a bear's food cache, slowly and quietly retreat. I've stumbled onto two different elk carcasses that bears had been feeding on, but the bruins must have either retreated or wandered off to get a drink, so I was able to get out of there without a confrontation. I simply made a big circle around the carcass and continued on my way without incident.

The needlesome thing about a black bear is that one bear will defend its food source, while another bear may run off at the sight of a human and return an hour later when it feels safe. Just because the last bear you encountered at a food cache ran away, don't take it for granted that the next black bear will do the same. Remember, black bears are powerful, unpredictable animals.

A Predatory Black Bear

Most black bears greatly fear humans and run away when

they become aware of a person nearby. However, it is fact that people have been stalked, killed and eaten by black bears who viewed them as prey. Some predatory black bear incidents have occurred near human habitations where the bears had become accustomed to humans and had lost their natural fear of man.

Several years ago, a black bear attacked a man and woman in a tent in a campground in what is now Rocky Mountain National Park. The bear bit the woman and then dragged the man off until other campers chased it away. The man died. The bear was later killed, and its belly was full of garbage.

The best way to avoid an encounter with a predatory black bear is to avoid areas of high human/bear activity, such as trails near resorts or garbage dumps. Also, learn where the large mammal birthing areas are located and plan to avoid those places because they may attract predatory black bears.

Keep The Dog At Home

Dogs and bears don't mix. A harassing dog may trigger a defensive protective response in a bear. Stories abound about dogs that ran ahead of their masters, got into trouble with a black bear, and then high-tailed it back to their owners — with the bear in close pursuit! However, a dog at home is a good sentinel to alert you that a marauding bear may be nearby.

HOW TO STOP A BLACK BEAR ATTACK
Don't Run!

The cardinal sin for any human who encounters a black bear is to run away. A bear may actually be spooked and ready to flee from a hiker, but a human running away may trigger an instinctive predatory reaction, prompting the bear to advance aggressively.

And forget that notion about running to a tree and climbing it. Black bears are excellent climbers, and aggressive black bears have pursued fleeing humans up trees and dragged them to the ground.

If a bear refuses to run off immediately, stand your ground and spread your arms out to appear larger. Make lots of noise and slowly back away. DO NOT CURL UP INTO A FETAL POSITION! A single black bear that advances aggressively toward a human, unlike a grizzly, is probably in a predatory mode, and you'll just be serving yourself up as a free meal. However, a sow with cubs is merely protecting her young, so a defenseless hiker who drops into a fetal position should be safe.

Sticks and Stones Often Do More Harm Than Good

There is some misinformation being circulated by word of mouth about the capability of a well-placed rock to drive off an aggressive bear. I once met two young men who were hiking in an area of high bear activity with no firearm or pepper spray, but they proudly displayed two hiking sticks and several hefty rocks that they planned to use on any bear that came near them. A bear has dense fur and seems to be immune to a three pound rock bouncing off its rump or noggin. If anything, it may serve to further antagonize a bear!

Years ago when I was stationed at a remote Forest Service ranger station, the cook asked me to get rid of three marauding black bears that were trying to break into the cookhouse. I didn't want to kill the bears if I could avoid it, so I waited in the kitchen that night, armed with a bow and blunt arrows.

A huge black bear showed up at dusk and I shot it at ten yards with a blunt arrow that should have raised quite a welt. The bruin ran off about twenty yards, but then turned back and ambled toward me. Two more blunts failed to faze the bear, and it began making false charges. Then I bounced three large rocks off its rump and ribcage. The bear continued forward, and I dove into the cookhouse. Meanwhile the bear began tearing at a side window.

My instructions were precise: Do anything necessary to stop those bears from damaging the building. I picked a spot between the bear's eyes and squeezed off a shot from my 30-30 rifle. The bear dropped in its tracks. I was forced to kill the two other bears on successive nights.

This sad story has two morals. First, a bear that becomes habituated to human food is a dangerous, unpredictable and, unfortunately, condemned animal. Second, sticks and stones usually have no effect on a determined bear and may actually prompt an attack.

Firearms

Not every black bear that stands its ground needs to be shot. A startled bear may woof a few times and stamp its front feet toward a hiker before it moves off. Also, a sow with cubs is sure to display some type of defensive aggression, such as making a short false charge, popping her teeth, or pacing back and forth while moaning menacingly.

However, a bear that advances within twenty yards should be considered a serious threat. Often times, a few shots over a black bear's head, or into the ground in front of it, will spook the bear and it will run off.

Try these diversionary tactics first, but if the bear continues

A black bear that advances toward a human should be viewed as a possible threat. Stand your ground, or slowly back away. Don't run, or you may trigger the bear's predatory instinct.

forward, you have every right to defend yourself. Aim between the eyes, and don't stop shooting until the bear is stopped.

Pepper Spray

Here's a classic example of a black bear's unpredictable nature. It's also a graphic illustration of what does, and doesn't, work on a predatory bear.

A Park Service ranger recently encountered a black bear on a trail in Glacier National Park. Bear and man met in a brushy area of limited sight distance, so the ranger wasn't too alarmed when the bear didn't run off. But then the bear became agitated and showed some signs of aggression. The ranger yelled and waved his arms, and the bear appeared to be moving off, but then began circling the man.

The ranger slowly retreated downhill off the trail, hoping that the bear might continue on its way if it was given the right-of-way. Instead, the bear stalked along the trail to the spot where the man had gone into the brush. The bear then left the trail, advancing toward the ranger with false charges and popping teeth. Its ears were laid back, a sure sign of aggression. The ranger bounced several large rocks off the bear, with no apparent effect. The bear came forward slowly, as if sizing up its quarry.

The good news is that the ranger was not defenseless. When the bear came within fifteen feet, the ranger blasted it in the face with pepper spray. The bear somersaulted backwards and turned to run, but slammed headfirst into a tree, momentarily stunning the bruin. The bear rolled over, madly pawing at its face, and then galloped off into the forest.

It raises the hair on the back of my neck whenever I recount the above story because that was a very dangerous black bear. Several recorded attacks that ended with humans being severely mauled or killed began with a black bear slowly working up its courage and then attacking.

Pepper spray works on black bears. It will not only keep you and your loved ones safe, but it will also administer a hot dose of adverse conditioning to a black bear that loses its fear of humans.

You can be sure that any bear shot in the face with pepper spray will react with fear and flee the next time it encounters a human. And here's a sobering thought: The alternative to pepper spray would be to face an oncoming bear with nothing.

BLACK BEAR QUICK-CHECK LIST

To Avoid A Black Bear Attack

1. Hike in a group.
2. Avoid brushy trails.
3. Make lots of noise to alert a bear to your presence.
4. Avoid trails near resorts or garbage dumps frequented by bears.
5. Stay out of big game birthing areas.
6. Avoid a bear's food cache or feeding area.
7. Store food 18 feet in a tree, but away from the trunk, and 100 yards from main camp.
8. Cook food 100 yards from main camp.
9. Use freeze dried foods in bear country, which have less odor.

To Stop A Black Bear Attack

1. Do not run away!
2. Do not try to climb a tree. Bears are excellent tree climbers.
3. Don't throw rocks at a bear. It may antagonize the bear.
4. Don't drop into a fetal position if a single bear attacks. It is in a predatory mode. Fight it off with feet, fists, sharp stick, fishing pole, etc.
5. Drop into a fetal position if a sow with cubs charges. She is in a defensive protective mode.
6. If armed with a gun, fire warning shots over the bear's head or in the dirt in front of it.
7. If a bear advances within 20 yards, consider it a threat to your safety.
8. If armed with pepper spray, shoot the bear when it gets within 30 feet. Start shooting at 60 feet if the bear is running at you.

Unlike the black bear, a grizzly bear may become aggressive when startled. (Photo courtesy Mike Pellegati.)

CHAPTER FIVE

The Grizzly Bear

Status

The grizzly bear has steadily increased in the past fifteen years to the point that consideration is being given by some to petition for its removal from the Endangered Species list. Biologists estimate about 1,200 grizzlies now live in the lower states, with about 20,000 in Canada and another 30,000 in Alaska. Most of the grizzlies in the lower states are located in Montana and Wyoming, but Idaho and Washington have also reported recent sightings.

Along with the increase in grizzly numbers has come a sharp increase in human/bear conflicts. The combination of more bears and more people living in some of the West's prime grizzly habitat has resulted in a very real threat to personal safety--for both man and bear!

It used to be that the couple hundred grizzly bears roaming the remote areas of the West were geographically separated by inaccessible wilderness from all but a handful of the most experienced, hardy travelers, and few conflicts arose. But in recent years, increased access by novices, increased recreation and increased bears have created a much greater potential for a grizzly encounter.

Grizzly Bear Behavior

The best way to describe a grizzly bear's personality is to consider a chance meeting between a 300 pound grizzly bear and a 300 pound black bear. The first reaction of the black bear would be to run away. The first impulse of the grizzly would be to charge the black bear, run it down and kill it. Then it would eat it, which is exactly what a mature grizzly will do to most black bears it can get its teeth into.

The purpose of the graphic illustration above is to point out the great difference between the temperament of a black bear and a grizzly. Hopefully, it will also serve as a reminder, even a warning, that grizzly bears are not to be taken lightly — ever.

I almost fell into this dangerous trap years ago when I encountered my first grizzly. I came around a bend in a trail and ran smack into a sow with two cubs about sixty yards away. I thought, "Oh, no! I'm in big trouble!" To my great relief, the sow ran off with her cubs.

I thought, "Maybe these grizzly bears aren't so dangerous after all." My next grizzly encounter changed my mind.

I was hiking through an alpine area next to a timbered ridge when I spotted a large grizzly pawing at some rocks 400 yards away. The bear was so far away that I doubted it could even see me, so I continued hiking along the ridge, expecting both parties to amiably avoid each other.

The wind shifted toward the bear, and the grizzly suddenly stood on its hind legs for a few seconds. Then it dropped to all fours and came galloping toward me. In a panic, I ran to a tree sixty yards away and had barely climbed up it when the grizzly was there, circling and popping its teeth. After a few minutes, it wandered off as if nothing had happened.

I believe that much of the danger concerning the grizzly is in our perception of this bear. A grizzly has short legs and a squat body that make it appear roly poly and slow. Also, it appears to affably amble through its habitat totally preoccupied with its own business. This often leads the uninitiated traveler to believe that if you treat the bear with respect and don't approach too close, it will leave you alone.

Big mistake. Two out of three grizzlies may behave exactly as above. The third grizzly will charge. That was the tragic case with a wildlife photographer in western Montana who had shadowed several grizzlies in the past, with no adverse reactions from the bears. One day he began shadowing a sow with two cubs. The last few frames in his camera at the site where searchers found his body showed the sow becoming increasingly agitated and then charging.

A grizzly will eat plants and grass to survive, but it prefers meat. In Glacier National Park, where fewer large mammals are available, a grizzly's diet consists of only 20 percent red meat. But in Yellowstone National Park, where large game herds roam, the grizzly's diet shoots up to 80 percent red meat.

A black bear may turn predatory in late spring during the birthing season, but the black bear does not have the speed or tenacity to take on a full grown bull moose or bull elk. On the other hand, a grizzly is "always" in a predatory mode and one horrible swipe from this powerful animal will drop the largest moose or elk in its tracks.

And as I mentioned before, a grizzly also looks upon his black bear cousin as fair game, A friend told me that he once watched a black bear feeding on a young elk carcass in Yellowstone. Presently, a medium-sized grizzly emerged from the timber above and caught the scent of the black bear and its kill. The grizzly made a slow stalk and pounced on the feeding black bear, killing it. Whereupon the contented griz spent the next few days dining on both prey and predator.

Grizzlies are even hard on each other, and a wayward cub runs the risk of ending up in a big old boar's belly. And here's another classic grizzly tale. During the early days of bear research in Yellowstone, the famed Craighead brothers related an incident about when they had shot a grizzly with a tranquilizer dart. The bear ran off about two hundred yards and then laid down. The researchers began driving toward the bear to study it. Suddenly, another grizzly charged out of the woods and killed the drugged bear with a bite to the back of the neck for no apparent reason other than predatory instinct.

The good news is that most grizzly bears instinctively fear man and will avoid humans if given the opportunity. It is a fact that very few grizzly attacks occur in bear country even though millions of people roam this habitat annually. Still, it's best to understand the unpredictable nature of this powerful predator and take the necessary steps to avoid it.

HOW TO AVOID A GRIZZLY BEAR

As with the black bear, the key to avoiding a grizzly is to know the four situations which often provoke a grizzly. They are: a startled grizzly, a hungry grizzly, a grizzly defending its food and a predatory grizzly. Many experienced wilderness travelers who venture into grizzly country every year, myself included, have very few problems with the Great Bear because they consciously work to avoid these four problem areas.

A Startled Grizzly Bear

Sixty percent of aggressive grizzly behavior results from a

The grizzly bear population has increased in recent years, leading to an increase in human/grizzly conflicts.

human and grizzly meeting at close quarters. While only an occasional black bear may act aggressive when startled, the majority of grizzlies will display aggression when suddenly confronted by a human. A startled sow with cubs is especially prone to charging, as a defensive protective action.

You should hike in grizzly country with the intention of never allowing dense brush to obscure your approach. I'll often circle a thicket and rejoin the trail a mile ahead in order to avoid dense cover in grizzly country.

Bear bells are also useful, but they don't carry well in undergrowth near gushing streams that tend to drown out the noise. It's best to yell or sing loudly as you enter thick cover. Do whatever it takes to let that bear know you're coming. Give it plenty of time to retreat without feeling threatened.

Also, there is great security in numbers in bear country. Bears don't like the odds stacked against them, and a half dozen petite women are enough to unsettle a big grizzly and send it packing. In Glacier National Park, it is common practice for a solitary hiker, or a pair of travelers, to school up with three or four other strangers and hike together.

A Hungry Grizzly Bear

There have probably been more than a million words written about the dangers of leaving food in camp, yet every year campers are injured by grizzly bears that were attracted to food left in camp. Grizzly bears are gluttonous opportunists, and if you leave food or food odors near camp, you're asking for a midnight visit from a grizzly.

Always hang your food at least eighteen feet up a tree and away from the trunk. Make sure this cache is at least a hundred yards from your sleeping camp, and plan to do your cooking at another site about a hundred yards from your main camp. Also, plan to eat freeze dried food. It has much less odor than smelly fish or bacon.

The Female Menstruation Problem In Grizzly Country

The subject of female hikers in their menstruation cycle is avoided by most bear experts. Some publications have even gone so far as to mention in passing that it has no relevance. Excuse me? A woman has an issuance of blood and body fluids that is heavy enough to require an absorbent pad, and we're supposed to believe that this acute predatory bear is going to respect this condition among human females because it is very personal in nature?

Without recounting the gory details of several incidents to the contrary, you should recognize this condition as potentially attractive to a grizzly, but a few simple precautions can alleviate the problem. If you are traveling co-ed, give your companions credit for some degree of maturity and inform them that you are having your period so they can give you extra privacy and freedom to stay odor free.

Plan to change your pad regularly, depending upon the flow of blood. Young girls issue very little blood in a four hour period, while older women who have had a few children often soak through a heavy sanitary pad after a few hours of physical activity. Change a saturated pad as often as necessary and place it in a waterproof sealing-type bag. You then have the option of burying it or carrying it along until you reach camp. You can then bury it far from camp. Before you go to sleep, change your pad and place it in two self-sealing bags, which should keep the odor locked inside. Do not throw it into the fire! Beside ruining the olfactory ambiance of the wilderness experience, the airborne odor will spread over a long distance.

A Grizzly Defending Its Food

Unlike the black bear, a grizzly is extremely dangerous while guarding its food cache. It is almost a certainty that you will be charged if the grizzly becomes aware of your presence, even at a hundred yards or more.

Never advance toward a grizzly guarding a carcass. If you should stumble upon a grizzly kill, slowly and quietly retreat. But make sure you alert a ranger or leave a note on the trail that a grizzly food cache lies ahead. In the national parks, rangers often have bear food caches marked, and they usually close all nearby trails until the bear has cleaned up the carcass and moved on.

A Predatory Grizzly

The best way to avoid a predatory grizzly bear is to avoid big game birthing areas where grizzlies may be hunting. Also, stay away from areas where grizzlies have been feeding on human garbage near dwellings. These bears have usually lost their natural fear of humans. Bear experts have traced many killer grizzlies back to dump sites where these bears had become habituated toward humans.

However, it remains a sobering fact that an occasional grizzly bear will look upon a human as prey. That's why vigilance is essential in grizzly country. A wary traveler should be able to detect an animal as large as a stalking grizzly. Many hikers have escaped predatory grizzlies by being alert and taking steps to thwart an attack.

Leave Your Dog At Home

Dogs are death in grizzly country — either for the dog or its master. A grizzly bear goes berserk when harassed by a yapping pooch and will quickly run it down and kill it if it can. Unfortunately, the dog often heads back to the security of its owner. Need I say more?

HOW TO STOP A GRIZZLY ATTACK

Running Away Sometimes Works!

Even though a fleeing human is sure to trigger a grizzly's predatory instincts, there are times when running may save a person's life, as it did once with me. If a bear charges from a distance, and a tree is close, you should run to the tree and climb it. Grizzlies have long claws and don't climb trees well, especially those with few limbs. But make sure you get at least fourteen feet up the tree.

Here's a story that'll make you shake your head. A wildlife biologist in Alaska's Mount McKinley National Park spotted a sow grizzly with two cubs a couple hundred yards away. Believe it or not, the man wanted to see how the sow would respond to a predator call, so he climbed a stunted spruce tree to about twelve feet off the ground and began calling. The sow became very agitated and ran in circles, frantically seeking the source of the screaming. She finally ended up under the tree and spotted the man.

The bear was able to clumsily climb up a few of the lower limbs, but that got her high enough to reach the man. She clamped onto his boot, dragged him from the tree and severely mauled him. The moral here is two-fold: A grizzly is the wrong animal to seek adventure with; and make sure you climb a tree that is tall enough to escape a grizzly.

If there is no tree nearby, or the advancing bear is too close, do not run! Stand your ground and avert your eyes. A grizzly will often make false charges, but then move away from a hiker who controls his impulse to flee.

Drop Into A Fetal Position

If the grizzly continues to advance, and you have no self defense, drop to the ground and curl into a fetal position with your hands clasped over the back of your neck. Many hikers have been sniffed and ignored, or cuffed and bitten a few times, while in this submissive position, but at least they escaped with their lives.

Don't Yell Or Throw Rocks

Yelling and throwing rocks at an animal such as a grizzly only serves to further agitate the bear and may even provoke it to charge. Instead, speak softly to an aggressive bear, and avert your eyes. Eye contact is an act of aggression in the wild kingdom.

Firearms

Not every grizzly that woofs and snaps its teeth at a hiker

Never approach a grizzly bear. Their short, squat appearance belies the fact that they are fast-moving, unpredictable and short tempered.

should be shot. Even a smallish grizzly may woof a few times, pop its teeth or make a false charge when disturbed, but most of these animals will eventually move off.

Also, a few shots over the bear's head, or into the ground in front of it, may convince the bear to leave, though a friend of mine told me that he once emptied his gun into a tree right above a grizzly's head, with no reaction at all from the bear. Then he found himself in the unnerving position of facing a grizzly at 15 yards with an empty gun! Fortunately, the bear eventually walked off.

Any firearm user should also be aware that the U.S. Fish & Wildlife Service investigates every grizzly shooting, and some trigger-happy folks have found themselves in big trouble for killing a protected grizzly without just cause.

Now for some more unsettling news. Carrying a firearm in grizzly country does not insure your safety. As strange as this may sound, there are times when gunfire may actually attract a grizzly. Hunters have returned from the woods with harrowing tales of grizzly bears actually coming on the run to the report of their rifles. The opportunistic grizzlies had begun to associate gunfire with a dead animal carcass!

A horrific example of this occurred a few years ago in British Columbia when two elk hunters failed to return to camp in the evening. Searchers found where the men had killed a bull elk. Evidence in the snow showed that the men were in the process of field dressing the elk and had placed their rifles about twenty feet away to keep them safe. A grizzly had stalked and killed both men before they could get to their rifles.

If you target practice in grizzly country, keep an eye peeled for this type of reaction from a grizzly.

Ultimately, you'll have to decide when a grizzly is too close. Some gun users have held off, even though a grizzly's false charge had stopped just ten yards away. Shooting a grizzly is serious business, but remember, you have a God-given right to defend yourself. If you decide to shoot, don't stop until the bear is down.

Pepper Spray

Nate Vance is a rawhide-tough outfitter who works in Wyoming's Thorofare Wilderness south of Yellowstone National Park. It's great elk country. It's also great grizzly country. One night, Nate walked out of his tent unprepared and walked right into a roaming grizzly. The bear swatted him, knocking him out and severely lacerating his head and face.

The next time Nate encountered an aggressive grizzly, he was prepared. His client had just shot an elk, and while Nate was gutting the animal, a grizzly charged out of the nearby brush. When the bear was twenty yards away and still coming, Nate blasted it with a hot dose of pepper spray. Nate said, "I've never seen a grizzly charge so fast, but then run away so fast!"

Nate added, "We used to keep all sorts of guns around camp, but I felt it didn't give the right message to folks. Here we were, saying that we liked the grizzly, yet we were armed to the teeth to kill it. Now, I have cans of pepper spray hanging in every corner instead of guns. We don't worry about bears too much anymore with the pepper spray."

There are still a few naysayers out there who publicly doubt the capability of a few ground up peppers to stop a huge charging grizzly. That's unfortunate; maybe even negligent. Whenever I read about some human being who was dragged out of a tent at night and killed by a grizzly, it fills me with great frustration because I always think, "That person's life could have been saved if they'd carried a can of pepper spray!"

There are simply too many testimonies by Park Service employees and other wilderness travelers about turning away charging grizzlies with pepper spray to ignore this self defense product. As for me, I'd rather hike grizzly country without my boots, than without my pepper spray.

GRIZZLY BEAR QUICK-CHECK LIST

To Avoid A Grizzly Attack
1. Hike in a group of at least four.
2. Avoid brushy trails.
3. Make lots of noise to alert a bear of your presence.
4. Avoid trails near resorts or garbage dumps frequented by bears.
5. Avoid big game birthing areas in late spring.
6. Keep food at least 100 yards from camp in a tree 18 feet from the ground and away from the tree trunk.
7. Cook food at least 100 yards from camp.
8. Avoid a bear's food cache or feeding area.

To Stop A Grizzly Attack
1. Run to a tree and climb it if the bear is not too close.
2. Don't run if a tree is not close by. This action triggers a grizzly's predatory instincts.
3. Don't throw rocks at a grizzly. It may prompt it to charge.
4. Avert your eyes. Eye contact is a form of aggression in the wild kingdom.

5. If unarmed and a grizzly charges, drop to ground and curl into a fetal position, hands over the back of your neck. Often times, a bear will just sniff you or bite a few times before moving on.

6. If armed with a gun, fire a few shots over the bear's head, or in the dirt in front of it to scare it away.

7. If armed with pepper spray, shoot the bear when it gets 30 feet away. Start shooting at 60 feet if the bear is running at you.

8. If armed, consider a bear within 20 yards to be a threat to your safety.

CHAPTER SIX

The Moose and Elk

Status

Moose and elk are large mammals whose numbers have increased dramatically in recent years. For instance, the elk population has doubled to a million animals in the past twenty years. Unfortunately, subdivisions are creeping into many areas where elk have historically roamed. Elk can be seen grazing in front yards or bedded down in the backyard. This has created a Utopian atmosphere for animal lovers, but it has also created problems for both elk and man.

Still, recent elk transplants to Wisconsin, Michigan, Arkansas, Kansas and Kentucky are cause for elk lovers to celebrate, but it's also time for folks who live in those areas to learn more about these large mammals.

Moose are thriving in those areas of suitable habitat in the West, upper Midwest and Maine. There are also large moose populations in Canada and Alaska. Their numbers are stabilized and the herd is healthy, though very little expansion is expected because of this large animal's specific habitat requirements.

Elk Behavior

Generally, an elk has a very mellow temperament and is very tolerant of humans. Summer vacationers in our national parks, where elk are not hunted, can often move within fifty yards without bothering a herd of elk. And therein lies the problem with the elk. That same bull elk that ignored you in August, may attack you during the September rut. And those cows that amiably fed

Many experienced backcountry travelers are as wary of the moose as they are of a bear.

while you watched them in May, may try to stomp you in June when their calves are born.

As you may have guessed, protective cow elk are responsible for the vast majority of elk related attacks on humans. You can't blame them. June is a killing field for newborn elk. Coyotes are trying to snatch away their babies, they're watching bears and lions carry off nearby calves, and they're not going to tolerate a photographer sneaking forward to get closeups of their babies.

Moose Behavior

Moose are solitary animals that don't like company. They seek out the more remote areas of their habitat, and they become upset when people move close to them. And unlike the elk, a moose is on edge twelve months each year. A moose attack is often unprovoked, and their huge hooves are lethal weapons. Consequently, hardened old-timers in Alaska consider the moose to be far more dangerous to encounter on a trail than a grizzly bear.

How To Avoid An Elk

Fortunately, elk like to feed in the open, and they even like to bed in open areas where they can keep watch for predators. Consequently, a human doesn't have to worry about stumbling into an angry elk.

However, many people do foolish things around elk because they think they're harmless. Not true. My records show that I've been treed by one grizzly bear and three elk! Heck, I've even been treed by cow elk!

Last spring, I was photographing a small herd of three cow elk and their calves in Yellowstone National Park. I was about a hundred yards away, which I considered a safe buffer distance that would not make the cows feel threatened. I was wrong.

The cows herded their calves together and made them lie down. Then one of the cows turned and looked directly at me. I knew what that meant! I slowly backed away, and the elk began slowly walking toward me. My pace increased, but so did the elk's. I ran to a nearby tree and looked back to see all three cows galloping toward me. I climbed the tree, and that seemed to confuse and justify the elk because they stomped back to their calves and seemed content after that. That's how unpredictable cow elk are when their calves are young.

It's easy to avoid an elk. In spring, don't get within a hundred yards of a cow with a calf. In the fall, don't get within a

A cow elk with calf in a National Park may become aggressive when approached. It's best to watch at a distance and avoid a confrontation.

A bull elk in the rut can become aggressive if you get too close.

hundred yards of a rutting bull elk, especially if he is guarding a harem of cows. I once watched a frantic Japanese tourist climb a light pole in Canada's Banff National Park because a rut-crazed bull elk had taken exception to his presence.

How To Avoid A Moose

Moose are big, surly animals. Even in the dead of winter they're dangerous. Occasionally, the Iditarod dog race in Alaska has a dog sled team that runs into a cow moose and gets pummeled. Moose can also be lethal. I watched a video showing a man on the outskirts of Anchorage, Alaska, get stomped and killed by a protective cow moose with calf.

The problem with moose is that they prefer to live and feed in dense brush, so a human hiking through a brushy area runs the risk of walking into a moose. If moose are present in the area you plan to hike, make lots of noise as you enter a brushy spot, or circle around the cover.

Do not approach a moose! Ever! This seems to trigger a protective defensive reaction from either a cow or bull. Even though cows are most dangerous in late spring when their young are born, and bulls during the fall rut, a moose may charge at any time of the year and should be avoided.

Dogs And Moose Don't Mix

Ask my wife, Aggie, about dogs and moose and she will emphatically inform you, "Dogs and moose don't mix!" She should know. A small dog that she'd taken on a short hike along a trail in northern Idaho scampered ahead and began barking. Aggie called the dog back. The dog came bounding back and ran between Aggie's feet.

That was the good news. The bad news was that a furious thousand pound cow moose also came back only three feet behind the terrified dog! The moose stood less than six feet away with the hair raised on her mane and angrily eyed Aggie for several minutes before slowly walking back up the trail.

Aggie was scared, but the dog was so frightened that it was

A cow moose is unpredictable at any time of year and should never be approached.

unable to walk. Aggie had to carry the terrified pooch all the way back to the vehicle. Aggie guessed that the dog had come upon a calf moose, and the cow had chased after the dog.

How To Stop An Elk Charge

Elk are preyed upon by a variety of large predators, so even when they act aggressive, they tend to become unnerved by counter-aggression. If an elk advances toward you, step forward, waving your arms and yelling loudly. Several times, I've had oncoming bull elk in rut turn and run away from this sudden action. Also, a nearby tree is a good source of escape, and you don't have to climb very high to make the elk turn and leave.

How To Stop A Moose Charge

Moose sometimes become very determined aggressors. Unlike an elk, an angry moose usually doesn't stop its charge when you begin yelling and waving your arms. A steady retreat often makes a moose cut short its charge, especially a bull. But if the moose continues coming fast and hard, run to a tree and climb it.

Firearms On Elk

It is not advisable to shoot an aggressive cow or bull elk. Most are just reacting to the threat of your presence, and if you get out of there fast enough, an elk will almost always break off its charge. Also, most elk are hunted. Even those that live in national parks get shot by hunters after they migrate out of these refuges. Consequently, a few shots over an elk's head will almost always send an aggressive elk packing.

Firearms On Moose

Iditarod racers carry rifles to protect themselves and their

It is a sad fact that bison injure more people in Yellowstone National Park than elk or moose. Never approach a bison. They may look ponderous and slow moving, but a bison may turn and attack a person who approaches too close.

dog teams from an attack by an angry moose in the trail. That should give you some idea of how potentially lethal a moose attack can be. If yelling, running, or shooting over a charging moose's head does not work, and the animal is within twenty yards and still coming, you have every right to defend yourself.

Pepper Spray

Pepper spray is a good deterrent to have handy if a moose or an elk charges you. If all other deterrent actions fail, look for a tree or bush to put between yourself and the oncoming elk or moose. If the animal does not go away, but acts aggressively, and tries to come around the tree after you, give it a shot of pepper spray. An elk or a moose will react the same way a lion or bear reacts to the fiery pepper sprayed into its face. It will depart immediately. Just remember to use your spray when the charging animal is still sixty feet away if you get caught out in the open.

Conclusion

Elk in the wild are hunted hard, and there is almost zero chance of getting attacked. Most attacks occur in national parks where elk are concentrated and have lost their instinctive fear of man. Even then, most humans are injured by elk as the result of foolhardy actions that most certainly could have been avoided.

Moose are also hunted in the wild, but they still are dangerous. Some hunters stalking moose have been forced to shoot in self defense when a bull moose became aware of their presence and charged. When the old-timers tell us that they're more wary of a moose than a grizzly, we should listen.

MOOSE AND ELK QUICK-CHECK LIST

To Avoid A Moose

1. Avoid brushy areas where moose like to live.
2. Make lots of noise to alert a moose to your presence.
3. Never approach a cow moose with a calf.
4. Be especially careful to avoid bull moose during the fall rut.

To Avoid An Elk

1. Never take it for granted that elk are docile. They are wild animals and act that way.
2. Do not approach cow elk with calves in spring, or rutting bulls in fall.

To Stop A Moose

1. If armed with a gun, shoot above the animal's head or into the ground in front of it. Step behind a tree and be ready to shoot if the animal continues onward within 20 yards. Use your judgment and be sure your life is in imminent danger before you kill the animal.
2. If armed with pepper spray, put a tree between yourself and the oncoming moose. If the animal continues to act aggressively and tries to come around the tree after you, spray it in the face with pepper spray.

To Stop An Elk

1. Quickly retreat, and the oncoming elk will usually break off its charge.
2. Climb a tree, and the elk will usually stop advancing.
3. Yell loudly, wave your arms. These aggressive actions usually stop an advancing elk.
4. If armed with a gun, shoot above the elk's head, or into the ground in front of it. It is very rare for an elk to continue onward after warning shots have been fired.
5. If armed with pepper spray, put a tree between yourself and the oncoming elk. If the animal continues to act aggressive and tries to come around the tree after you, spray it in the face with pepper spray.

CHAPTER SEVEN

Poisonous Snakes

Status

Most of the poisonous snakes found in the lower 48 states are rattlesnakes, with three species being non-rattling, such as the copperhead, water moccasin and coral snake. A biology book can fulfill your academic curiosity about scientific data. This book will instead focus on snake activity and awareness to make sure you don't have to learn firsthand about the dangers of a particular snake's venom.

Snakes are feared more than any other wild creature in the world. For most folks, a snake appears as the embodiment of evil as it slithers along the ground with tongue flickering in and out. However, snakes are neither evil, nor nice. They are just another animal species that does its part in balancing the cycle of nature. Indeed, snakes are the great eliminators of pests in America. Smaller snakes eat insects, while larger snakes eat untold millions of rodents that would soon overpopulate the world if left unchecked.

Of course, this is all a moot point to the nature lover who fears being bitten by a poisonous snake. The good news is that you can hike and camp throughout snake country safely if you learn where snakes live and hide.

I was once hysterically fearful of snakes. If I knew that poisonous snakes (even one!) existed in a certain area, I would not walk there. As a videographer, I was once assigned to record a professional snake catcher as he removed rattlesnakes from several dens. I was terrified!

But I soon learned that snakes were relatively easy to avoid if you paid attention to where you put your feet. By the end of the first day, I had poisonous snakes slithering all around me, and I quickly lost my fear of these serpents when it became obvious that they were much more frightened of me!

Snake Behavior

Snakes are cold blooded members of the reptile family and have no way to regulate their body temperature. A temperature of 105 degrees will kill a snake, and a temperature of 50 degrees will cause it to go into hibernation. On a hot sunny day, you simply will not find a snake in the open. They must seek the shade of a rock or bush to escape the radiant heat of the day.

A snake hunts by using its tongue to "taste" the air for the scent of a rodent. The snake slowly slithers along the ground flickering its tongue out to taste its way to a mouse or rat. A snake can also detect movement by vibration. A man's footfall fifteen feet away will be detected by a snake. I've had snakes scurry away when I was still thirty feet away by sensing the vibrations of my footfalls.

The problem for humans is that a poisonous snake simply reacts. It has no reasoning power, so when a hiker walks within range of a snake, its first reaction is to flee when it feels threatened. If it can't flee, it may warn the nearby trespasser by rattling or hissing. If that doesn't work, it may strike.

How to Avoid Snakes

It is very important to understand one very large principle of snake behavior. There is not one snake in America that will seek out a human and try to bite him or her. Not one! If you are careful to make noise, watch where you put your hands and feet, and practice snake awareness, you should never have a serious problem in snake country.

The key to avoiding a snake is to understand that most snakes hunt during the evening or night, when the hot sun won't harm them. If you avoid hiking in late evening or night, you will avoid the prime snake movement time periods and thereby reduce your chances of encountering a poisonous snake by 60 percent.

Come morning, most snakes seek shelter to escape the heat of the sun. They crawl under rocks, logs, and brush in the woods, and they'll stay there until the heat of the day subsides. You should avoid walking through dense brush in snake country, stay

Poisonous snakes are found in every state in the lower 48 states. But if you know how a snake lives and where it likes to hide, you should be able to avoid these serpents and safely enjoy your time afield. (Photo courtesy Gary Holmes.)

away from rock piles, and never step over a log without first checking for a snake. By strict adherence to the above precautions, plus not hiking late in the evening, you'll reduce your chances of encountering a poisonous snake to almost zero. Break any of the above rules, and your chances of encountering a snake rise sharply, as Harvey Mead found out.

Harvey was only 12 years old when he climbed a small rock outcrop while playing a game of tag with a friend. Harvey told me, "I grabbed the top rock to pull myself up and felt a sharp bee sting on my right hand. I pulled back and circled the rock outcrop to see where the bee's nest was located. That's when I saw a rattlesnake crawling away. I got sick for a few days, but then I was over it."

Unfortunately, not all kids are as lucky as Harvey Mead. Poisonous snakes kill more than a dozen people annually, and most of them are children whose small bodies are not able to withstand the ravages of snake poison. For that reason, children especially should be educated about where and how poisonous snakes live.

The one exception to the above precaution is the water moccasin, a snake that lives in the swamps of the South. This snake is largely aquatic and rests on logs or along grassy shorelines. If you live in moccasin country, be very careful where you place your feet and hands while swimming or fishing.

Also, avoid taking your boat past overhanging tree limbs. Moccasins often crawl onto these limbs to rest and hunt. More than one fishermen has surprised a dozing moccasin, and the snake jumped from the limb right into the boat! Whereupon it became very aggressive, and serious snake bites have resulted. In moccasin country, stay in the open and away from grassy shores, logs, cypress trees and overhanging limbs.

If you are nervous about hiking through snake country, or if you'll be moving through dense undergrowth, it might be wise to wear snake-proof chaps, or purchase a pair of specially constructed snake-proof boots. These are gaining in popularity among sportsmen who must walk through snake areas in the dark on their way to and from hunting or fishing.

Poisonous Snakes of North America

The purpose of this special section is to help the reader identify the various poisonous snakes in each region of the country and understand the danger of an encounter. Not all poisonous snakes carry the same amount and potency in their venom, making certain snakes far more dangerous than others.

Copperhead

The copperhead is a forest and field dwelling snake of the eastern states, but its range extends all the way down to Texas. Here's the bad news about copperheads. They are so well camouflaged that a copperhead lying in leaves is very difficult to spot. Consequently, several thousand people are bitten by copperheads annually. The good news is that copperheads are shy, docile snakes who's venom is low in toxicity. Very few deaths occur from copperheads.

I grew up in copperhead country in Pennsylvania, and I only encountered one of these serpents. I began poking at it with a stick, and it took much prodding before the snake struck. Most copperhead bites occur when this well camouflaged reptile is stepped on, or when folks carelessly handle boards or brush without first checking for snakes.

Cottonmouth

The cottonmouth is a charcoal colored snake with a thick body and no rattles. It inhabits swampy country throughout the lower Mississippi Valley up to southern Illinois, and from Florida northward to Virginia. When surprised or disturbed, a water moccasin, or cottonmouth, often defends itself aggressively. This snake is surly and lethal, and it should be avoided.

Timber Rattlesnake

The timber rattler is found from New York south to Georgia and westward into Illinois, Arkansas, Missouri and Kansas. The timber rattler's venom is highly toxic, but this snake is generally not very aggressive. It likes to live in timbered lands

In snake country, stay away from rocky areas or downed logs or dense brush. These are places where snakes tend to hide during the day to escape the sun's heat. (Photo courtesy Gary Holmes.)

and hides under logs and in rocky brush piles. While this snake is not high on the list of dangerous snakes, it should be avoided and watched for throughout its habitat. It is especially bad when new rural subdivisions are carved out of timbered areas in the East. For the first few years, timber rattlers are often found near these new dwellings.

Eastern Diamondback

The eastern diamondback rattlesnake is the most dangerous venomous snake in America because it can grow up to nine feet in length with 1½-inch fangs. It can deliver a large amount of highly toxic venom in its bite. Its range extends from the coastal plains of the Carolinas south to Florida and Louisiana.

In some areas of Florida, undergrowth flourishes. A hiker should avoid such areas because snakes curl up under these bushes, and if you cannot see a safe place to put your feet, and have no open areas to walk through, you have no business pushing through these snake havens.

Western Diamondback

The western diamondback rattlesnake is responsible for more deaths annually than any other poisonous snake. That's because it is numerous and, at eight feet in length, almost as large as its eastern cousin. It is also much more irritable and aggressive. It will attempt to retreat at first, but then it will strike repeatedly at its adversary. Its range extends through Texas, Arizona, New Mexico, Oklahoma, and Arkansas. Because this is hot, dry country, the eastern diamondback will always by hidden under a rock or bush during the heat of the day, allowing plenty of room for a traveler to avoid it.

Prairie Rattlesnake

This snake covers a huge range of open prairie all the way from Texas northward into Canada, including the Dakotas, Kansas and Nebraska. It grows to five feet or more and is very numerous in some areas. It is not overly aggressive and the open nature of the prairie allows a hiker plenty of room to avoid typical rocky areas where these snakes like to escape the heat of the day.

Coral Snake

The coral snake is the only member of the cobra family in North America. This brightly colored snake has yellow, black and red bands around its slim, three-foot-long body. Its venom is far more potent than a rattlesnake's venom. However, it injects a minute amount of venom in its bite, and it is not an aggressive snake. In fact, its mouth is so small that it is capable of biting a human only on a finger. Still, this snake should be respected and avoided because of its potential.

How to Stop a Snake Attack

Here's a chilling scenario to consider. You notice a buzzing sound in the bushes to your left. You glance down and a jolt of adrenalin scorches through your body. A rattlesnake is coiled just three feet from your leg. What should you do? Run? Kick at the snake? Pick up a rock and throw it? Or just stand there and hope the snake doesn't strike?

Hopefully, you will have been observant and careful in snake country so that the above scenario will never happen. But sometimes, a lapse in caution may occur, and it's best to know what to do when a snake is suddenly within striking distance.

After I lost my unreasonable fear of snakes while filming the snake handler, I began experimenting with individual snakes. I was wearing snake-proof chaps so I purposely placed my foot within striking distance of several snakes that had been disturbed. To my surprise, not every snake that rattled and coiled struck at my leg. In fact, of the seven snakes that I provoked, only two struck at me, and only one of those snake's fangs actually hit my chap.

I discovered that if I stood still, and the snake still had room to retreat, the serpent began a slow, defensive movement backward, even as it was coiled and its head was reared and ready to strike, until it actually moved beyond striking range. (Generally, a snake can strike forward about two-thirds of its body length. Most snakes measure about two to four feet in length.)

Here's another interesting observation. The snake that struck my leg chap did not penetrate the outer canvas material, which led me to study several snake books until I discovered that only about one-third of snake strikes actually inject venom into a human. The other strikes either had the snake's mouth already closing, or it was a "dry" bite, meaning that the muscles surrounding the venom sack did not activate in time to force the poison up through the hypodermic fangs while they were penetrating the skin.

I then began experimenting with the idea of putting something between my leg and the coiled snake. Three times, I dropped a glove on the ground a foot from the snake. The rattling intensified, and the snake coiled more menacingly, but it was apparent that the glove had the desired effect of distracting the snake away from my leg and to the glove. Interestingly, none of the snakes struck at the glove. I believe that they sensed it was inanimate, and its stationary position further allayed their fears. They did begin to back up, though.

I then placed a walking stick between my leg and two coiled snakes. Both times, the stick caused an increased warning, but it had the desired effect of taking the snake's attention from my leg, and both times I was able to move my leg without a strike.

I realize that my tests were impromptu and rough, but they showed me that a walking stick is a valuable tool in snake country. You can beat the bushes with it to scare away any hidden snakes, or you can use it to dispatch a snake. I also believe that if you find yourself in the unenviable position of discovering a coiled snake within striking distance, a walking stick placed directly between your leg and the snake can help you avoid being struck.

On another occasion, I did some experimenting with snake chaps to see what it took to get a snake to strike. Three times, I stood within striking distance (three feet) of coiled prairie rattlesnakes, and none of them struck at me when I moved my leg six inches closer, but after I'd moved within two feet, all three snakes struck at my chaps, with two snakes actually placing their fangs into the outer canvas fabric. From this rough experiment, I deduced that the closer you get to a snake within its striking distance, the greater your chances of being struck and having venom injected in you.

From these experiments, I've come up with a list of suggestions to avoid being struck by a snake. First, stay still if you discover a snake within striking distance. Carry a walking stick and place it between yourself and the snake, or drop some item in front of the snake. Allow the reptile to retreat without moving your leg. Remember, the snake is in a defensive protective position and will strike only to defend itself.

Wear heavy clothing and heavy leather boots in snake country. Snake chaps are not a bad idea if you have to enter certain areas of heavy undergrowth where visual snake detection

Trim back dense underbrush and high grass from around your house to keep snakes from seeking shelter there. (Photo courtesy David Biddlecome.)

not possible.

Treating a Snake Bite

In the old days, we were instructed to slice deep into both fang puncture wounds and suck out the poison. This procedure has been proven useless, since the venom is already in the bloodstream, and you'll just create a greater injury by slicing into the muscle tissue with a knife. The most effective treatment for snakebite is to keep the victim calm, thereby slowing the spread of the poison, and then seek medical help quickly.

Most hospitals in snake country carry a supply of snake anti-venom. This serum is developed by injecting a horse with gradually increasing doses of snake venom until the horse's body has built up an immunity to it. Some of the horse's blood is then drawn and separated to be used as anti-venom.

If you or someone else is bitten by a snake, clean the wound and ice it down. Get to a hospital as soon as possible. Most snakebite victims who receive anti-venom shots within a few hours of being bit rapidly recover with no ill effects.

POISONOUS SNAKE QUICK-CHECK LIST

How To Avoid A Poisonous Snake

1. Educate children where and why snakes live in your area.
2. Never allow children to scamper around brush, high grass or rocks in snake country.
3. Avoid walking in snake country in late evening or night, when the snakes emerge to hunt.
4. Avoid walking through brush and high grass, near bushes, or among rocks where snakes tend to hide during the day.
5. Never place your hand or foot on a rock or log without first checking for a snake behind or under it.
6. Never step over a rock or log without first checking behind and under it for a snake.
7. Wear heavy boots or snake proof chaps, especially if you must move through dense brush, high grass, or rocky areas where it will

not always be possible to see a snake in front of you.

8. If you intend to camp in snake country, plan to sleep on a portable cot, which will keep you above the ground and away from any snakes traveling through during the night.

How To Avoid Being Bit By A Poisonous Snake

1. Do not move if you discover a coiled snake within a few feet of your leg.

2. Place a hiking stick or drop an object between yourself and the snake.

3. Quickly remove your leg or hand as soon as the snake is distracted.

4. Allow a slowly retreating snake to move out of striking range.

5. Wear snake-proof chaps or boots.

What To Do If You Are Bitten By a Snake

1. Remain calm. Limit physical activity to lessen the spread of venom through the blood stream.

2. Wash the puncture wounds to remove surface venom and avoid infection.

3. Get to a hospital as soon as possible to receive a shot of snake anti-venom.

CHAPTER EIGHT

Poisonous Spiders and Scorpions

Spider Status

All spiders are poisonous. They are highly efficient predators who kill their insect prey by injecting venom through fang bites. However, the vast majority of spiders are either too small to bite through the skin of a human, or carry weak venom that is not strong enough to affect a human.

There are three spiders that have the potential to harm a human, but only two of them pose a serious threat to man's safety. The tarantula is the biggest, scariest American spider, but it is a rather docile arachnid. In fact, many are kept as pets. A gentle handler can actually pick up a tarantula and allow it to walk all over the person without fear of being bit.

The other two poisonous spiders are a different story. The black widow and brown recluse spiders are large enough to inject a dangerous dose of poison into a human, and special precautions should be taken to avoid these spiders.

Scorpion Status

There are many scorpion species, ranging from inch-long miniatures to specimens up to eight inches long. All carry venom in their overhead stingers. Surprisingly, some smaller scorpions carry much more toxic venom, but their tiny size keeps them from injecting very much of it. Generally, you can tell how venomous a scorpion's sting is by the size of its pinchers. A scorpion with smaller claws will have a more lethal dose of venom in its stinger.

The scorpion community revolves around a vicious cycle of cannibalism. Though a scorpion may prey on any insect that comes near, most scorpions prey on other smaller scorpions. Scorpions are limited to a hot dry climate, so their range is not expanding. States such as Arizona, New Mexico, Nevada, Texas and California all have large scorpion populations, though a few scorpions are located as far north as southern Canada.

Tarantula Behavior

The tarantula is a spider of the hot, dry Southwest. They are common in the desert, vacant lots and backyards, where they hunt insects and generally cause great fear among visitors, but rarely more than a glance from local residents. Tarantulas live under garbage piles, old sheds, or in holes. They are a semi-trapdoor spider that springs out of cover at their prey. That's one reason why tarantulas cause fear among humans. A tarantula that

The Tarantula is the largest spider in North America. Its bite is usually painful, but not serious. It's often kept as a pet and bites only when mishandled or alarmed. (Photo courtesy Mike Pellegatti.)

senses a disturbance outside its lair will suddenly spring forward toward a nearby human, expecting it to be an insect. The startled human, who thinks he is being attacked, reacts by stomping the poor spider.

A tarantula can deliver a painful bite, resembling a bee sting, from its large fangs. A human will feel quite a bit of discomfort at first, but this spider's venom is not very powerful and only local swelling usually results. Most tarantula bites result from rough handling, or when the spider is alarmed.

Black Widow Behavior

A mature black widow spider is best known for the distinctive red hourglass design on her belly. An immature widow's body may be red or brown and does not become black until it reaches maturity, making it sometimes difficult to see the hourglass design on one of these younger pea-sized widows. Besides, you really don't need to risk being bit by turning a widow onto her belly to identify her. A widow's body is very distinctive with its large, bulbous thorax (body), small head and long legs.

The black widow is a web spider who waits at its edge for an insect to be caught in the sticky filaments. The widow is especially numerous in the southern states where temperate weather and a profusion of insects create optimum conditions. In many areas of the Southwest, just about every piece of garbage or woodpile will be infested with black widows.

This spider's first impulse is to run for the safety of cover when discovered. A black widow is not aggressive, and any disturbance causes her to attempt an escape, often curling up and feigning death. However, when escape is not possible, the widow will turn and face its tormenter in a defensive protective position, with its front legs extended and ready to bite.

I once placed a captured black widow into a small box to experiment with it. I donned a heavy leather glove and began putting the index finger close to the spider. Each time the black widow tried to escape, until the finger came close, whereupon it would rear up and prepare to defend itself. Finally, I moved the tip of the gloved finger a half-inch away. As soon as its front legs felt the finger, the black widow lunged forward and bit into the glove. The spider lingered there for about two seconds while it injected its venom. Then it retreated a short distance and readied to defend itself again.

Black widow spiders are extremely numerous in some southern states, and the incidence of widow bites shows it. Annually in southern California, there are about 400 reported black widow bites.

Curiously, male humans are bitten seven times more often than females. The reason for this becomes painfully clear when you consider the fact that most of these bites occur in outhouses where black widows weave nests below the seat to catch flies attracted by the human waste. A man's sex organs extend below the seat, and if they make contact with the web, a black widow

The black widow is the most common highly venomous spider in North America. Lumber piles, outhouses and crawl spaces under houses or trailers are favorite hiding places for the widow. (Photo courtesy John Reid.)

will rush over and bite anything that makes the web vibrate. Indeed, the majority of black widow bites on men are on the penis.

The widow is truly an adaptable spider. It now lives not only in the southern states, but has also extended its range to the cold northern states. Today, the black widow is found in every lower state.

Brown Recluse Behavior

The brown recluse originated in South America and arrived in North America in cargo. It likes warm, moist habitat and is found in most of the southern states where temperatures are moderate. Most northern states have been free of this large brown spider, but in recent years, it has extended its range northward to several midwest and eastern states.

The brown recluse, often called a fiddleback because of a

Don Witty felt fortunate to be well enough to hold his newborn baby shortly after he was bitten by a brown recluse spider. Note the extreme swelling in his bandaged hand. Photo courtesy Don Witty.)

dark brown fiddle shape on its head, does not live in a web, but prefers a lair, such as a crack in a sidewalk or the space between pieces of wood. Recluse spiders also do much of their hunting among the foliage of plants and trees. This spider likes privacy and solitude, hence the term recluse.

The recluse is a very dangerous spider that becomes aggressive when disturbed. Numerous serious bites, and a few deaths, occur annually from this dangerous arachnid.

Scorpion Behavior

Scorpions hunt mostly at night to escape the desert heat. Before daylight, a scorpion will retreat under a cool rock at a dry creek bed or a pile of rubbish. When disturbed, a scorpion will run away, and they are surprisingly fast. However, when cornered, a scorpion will turn and face its aggressor. Its wicked stinger is quick to spring forward, and it will sometimes turn into the aggressor as it makes short rushes at its adversary. A scorpion's sting is very painful, and there have been a few fatalities, especially to smaller children.

How to Avoid a Tarantula

Because of its size, the tarantula is fairly easy to avoid. If you don't try to pick one up or squeeze it, you should never have a problem with this large spider. When hiking or camping in the Southwest, shake your clothing out and check your boots or shoes for any tarantula that may have sought safety there.

How to Avoid a Black Widow Spider

Black widow spiders are everywhere insects are found. Unfortunately, human dwellings are excellent breeding grounds for insects, and widow spiders follow them there. However, a widow can be found just about anywhere bugs and protective cover are found.

Alan Landers was on a camping trip in the Scapegoat Wilderness Area of western Montana — a remote alpine backcountry where deep snow and bitter cold are common in winter. Obviously, this is not a place where a guy expects to encounter a black widow.

When Alan turned over in his sleeping bag, he felt a slight stinging sensation on the side of his neck. He slapped at it and figured he had killed a big mosquito. In a few minutes, the bite area became itchy, and then sore. Within a half hour, Alan was nauseous and feverish. He was too sick to help break camp and had to be helped out of the woods by his friends. He remained sick for two days, with a high fever and chills, but all effects of the black widow bite disappeared after that.

Alan's experience is typical of a black widow bite. While painful and troublesome, a widow's bite is rarely fatal. Fatalities are rare from widow bites, occurring mostly among small children or people who have an allergic reaction to the widow venom.

Most widow bites occur when human skin inadvertently makes contact with a widow, and the alarmed spider bites in self defense. A widow hunts at night, and by dawn, it retreats into a dark place to hide. This dark place may be inside a pant leg or shirt sleeve. Shoes are also favorite widow hiding places. In addition, widows like the dark musty areas under a building's foundation, and they especially seem to thrive under trailer houses.

I would suggest that anyone who purchases a home in spider country should plan to set off a few spider bombs in advance of any cleaning chores. These potent devices exude a strong spider insecticide that will seep into all those nooks and crannies where a venomous spider may be hiding.

It's also a good idea to give your clothes a shake before putting them on, especially if they are hanging on a porch outside, or garage, etc. Also, I've gotten into the habit of stomping on the toes of any shoes left outside, after I once shook a black widow out of a boot I was preparing to put on.

If you must go into a dark area, such as the crawl space under your house, take it for granted that a few widows will be residing there. Plan to wear gloves and heavy clothing that a spider could not bite through. I've also gotten into the habit of wearing cotton gloves while doing chores around my Montana home if I intend to be moving boards or pulling out stacked items from dark places where a widow may be hiding.

How to Avoid a Brown Recluse

Annette Harris is a school teacher who had just left a meeting in Pomona, California, when she dropped her keys into an empty flower pot outside the building. She retrieved her keys and hopped into her vehicle and drove off.

A half hour later, the palm of her hand became itchy and red. An hour later it became swollen and painful. She had a doctor look at it, and he immediately identified it as a brown recluse bite. He gave Annette antibiotics and instructed her to go home and elevate the arm.

But several hours later, Annette's condition had worsened and she went to the emergency room, where a toxologist tried everything possible to save her rapidly deteriorating hand. In less than a day, gangrene had already begun to develop in the toxin-laced fluid in her hand. One finger turned blue, then black. Gangrene had set in, and doctors decided to remove it, hoping to save her hand.

With the gangrous finger removed, medical experts were able to save Annette's hand, but she experienced several other side effects from the brown recluse bite. Annette was fortunate. Several people each year die from recluse bites that were not reported to medical experts promptly. The main culprit is gangrene, which spreads rapidly through the infected area.

If you live in a state that harbors the brown recluse, plan to periodically "spider bomb" your house or have a pest control expert spray it. Also, educate your children about the recluse and instruct them on how to avoid this very dangerous spider. Check your shoes before you stick a toe in them. I usually stomp on the toe. And make sure you shake out your clothing each morning. My next door neighbor, Tim Barnes, did and it may have saved his life!

Tim recently traveled to southern California with his National Guard unit. One night, they were scheduled to sleep out.

The sergeant advised everyone to shake out their boots and clothes in the morning before they dressed. Next morning, Tim awoke and shook out his boots. Nothing. Then he shook his pants, and a huge brown recluse came tumbling out of a pant leg!

It's also a good idea to wear gloves when handling piled boards, brush, tree limbs or other objects where a recluse may seek seclusion, but make sure your gloves have a knit wrist to avoid a recluse getting at the exposed skin behind the cuff. Los Angeles fireman Don Witty was fighting a garbage fire in a vacant lot while wearing standard cuffed gloves. While overturning junk boards to get at the smoldering fire, Don felt a slight prick to the back of his hand and slapped at it, thinking it was just a small spark. An hour later, his hand was red, swollen and painful.

The hospital emergency room personnel guessed it was a recluse bite and rushed him to an entomologist. Antibiotics and anti-gangrene medicine at first failed to stop the spread of the poison. Don's hand and arm swelled up like a balloon, and at one point his fingers actually looked webbed. It took intense medical attention to save his arm. This story's moral is to avoid wearing cuffed gloves that might allow a spider to fall in behind the cuff.

How to Avoid a Scorpion

Scorpions like to seek secluded areas to hide from other predators (usually bigger scorpions!) and escape the hot sun. A rock is a good scorpion hiding place, but so is a boot or a pair of pants. The best way to avoid the painful sting of a scorpion is to be very careful donning clothes left on the ground or floor in scorpion country. Always shake out your boots, and I would suggest also stomping on them a few times to squash any scorpion hiding inside.

Also, don't handle trash or junk lumber with your bare hands. Always use heavy leather gloves with a knit wrist. Don't just walk up to a rock and sit on it because a scorpion hiding underneath may react defensively. While climbing, don't place your hand on a rock without first checking to see if a scorpion could be hiding underneath it.

Conclusion

The vast majority of spiders are not a danger to humans. The tarantula and scorpion can inflict a painful bite if harassed. The widow and recluse spiders carry dangerous doses of venom and should be avoided. Diligence is the key in spider country. Even though the bite of these two spiders is very toxic, their fangs are small. The danger here is that many folks are unaware that they were even bitten.

If you experience the classic symptoms of a venomous spider bite, such as itching, redness, swelling, and intense localized pain, get to a medical facility quickly. With a neurotoxin, the sooner the better.

ARACHNIDS QUICK-CHECK LIST
How to Avoid a Poisonous Spider Bite

1. Bug bomb your home and the crawlspace below periodically.
2. Spray insecticide along the foundation of your home to keep insects and spiders away.
3. Avoid large brush or lumber piles near the house or backyard.
4. Always handle brush or lumber with gloves to avoid being bit by a spider hiding there.
5. Cut down high grass near backyard play areas to discourage spiders from living close to human activity.
6. Never place your hands in places where a spider may be hiding, inside or outside the home.
7. Periodically, spray dark closets and under each bed to eliminate indoor spiders hiding in these dark places.
8. Do not allow clothing, toys, or other items to remain piled on the floor. These are easy hiding places for spiders.
9. Always shake your clothes out before putting them on, specially if they were hung outside or in the garage.
10. Stomp on the toe of your shoes or boots to kill any spiders that may have climbed into these dark places overnight.
11. In spider country, plan to use a cot to sleep on to get your body above the ground where a spider might pass through during the night.

How To Avoid A Scorpion Sting

1. Never sit or place your hand on a rock or log without first checking for a scorpion hiding underneath.
2. In scorpion country, plan to use a cot when sleeping to get your body above the ground where a scorpion might pass through in the night.
4. Always shake out clothing left on the ground overnight before you put it on.
5. Always shake out your boots, or stomp on them, to avoid any scorpion who climbed in during the night.

A scorpion can deliver a painful sting. Avoid rocks and logs in scorpion country. Campers should shake out their clothes and boots in the morning to expose any scorpion that may have hidden there during the night. (Photo courtesy Mike Pellegatti.)

Alligators have increased rapidly in the past two decades. So have complaints. View these large reptiles at a safe distance. (Photo courtesy Mike Pellegatti.)

CHAPTER NINE

The Alligator

Alligators pose a potential threat to outdoors people within a relatively small geographical region, but in these specific areas, the threat and the danger are very real. Florida resident Chuck Cannon is no stranger to danger. Chuck works for the Orlando Police Department in its anti-drug section. Yet he feels safer at his job than he does on the nearby St. Johns River. The reason? Gators!

Chuck told me, "When I was a kid, you could swim in the St. Johns river without fear of gators. There were a few around, and they were fun to watch, but hunters kept their numbers down to a manageable level. The state cut way back on gator hunting and today there are so many big gators out there that I won't take my family out on the water. I took my wife out for a short boat ride this past spring, and we saw more than a dozen 13 foot alligators. Those things are huge! They're aggressive and always hungry."

Chuck added, "I used to love to hunt ducks in the marshes around the house. Not any more. There are so many gators that they get the ducks I shoot before I can get to them. A couple times, my black lab barely beat a gator back to the boat. I quit duck hunting when the gators started eating my decoys."

Status

Alligators are found in those southeastern states below 35 degrees north latitude — mainly Florida, Louisiana and Mississippi, though several neighboring states also have small populations. These huge, powerful reptiles have the potential to inflict horrible injuries to humans, and even a few deaths have been recorded. As much fear and concern as the growing mountain lion population has created throughout the West, it is a fact that alligators complaints far exceed lion complaints. In central Florida alone, about 5,000 alligator complaints are lodged annually.

Once driven to the brink of extinction by poaching for their hides, the alligator was placed on the Endangered Species List, and an ambitious restocking program was begun in the 1970's. To say that this program was a success would be an understatement. In Florida alone, there are now an estimated one million alligators, and this species has since been removed from the Endangered Species List. Very limited hunting is now allowed, but the pendulum has swung the other way, with large overpopulations of this prolific reptile in many places where gators were absent a dozen years ago.

Alligator Behavior

Alligators are water reptiles that can reach a length of thirteen feet and weigh more than 600 pounds. They carry a huge set of wicked teeth in their powerful jaws. And being reptiles, gators act instinctively. An Everglades guide commented that gators have only two thoughts in their heads at all times: "Can I eat it, or can it eat me!"

Alligators subsist mainly on rough fish or carrion in the tepid backwaters and marshes where plenty of water vegetation hide them from prey and predator alike. They lie immobile for hours in marsh grass with only their eyes and nose poking above the water. When a fish, small mammal or duck swims by they lunge at it and swallow it whole. A hungry alligator will also attack larger mammals. With large prey, the gator clamps onto a section of flesh and then spins its body furiously until the flesh is torn away.

How to Avoid An Alligator

Ray Ginn is a professional alligator trapper for the state of Florida. Ray told me, "The number one cause of alligator problems in Florida is tourists feeding them. Gators are instinctively fearful of man. I believe a man's erect stature confuses and intimidates a gator, so most want to run away at the sight of a tall human — unless they become acclimated to people."

Ray continued, "Tourists flock to these gator areas and feed them bread and marshmallows. The gators begin to associate humans with food, and when there is no easy food to eat, a gator may look upon that human as its next meal. Also, gators are reactionary if too many people get around them and if a kid surprises one, it may instinctively snap. That's when most of the serious injuries occur."

The best way to avoid an alligator attack is to stay away from those areas where gators tend to congregate, especially grassy swamps where lots of water vegetation may hide the gators. An alligator expert mentioned that the best time for people to be out in gator country is during the mid-day heat of summer. The gators retreat because they can't stand the heat, and they won't emerge into the open until evening.

It is an unnerving spectacle to see a large alligator lying on a log, seemingly waiting to attack anything that wanders by. Though this is a malicious sight, the fact is that the alligator is merely using the heat from the sun to digest its food. If you approach one of these gators, it will usually slip into the water and retreat.

In late summer, a pregnant female alligator will lay her eggs in a scraped up pile of mud and vegetation that resembles a muskrat hut. A person should avoid these humped up mounds because a female alligator is very aggressive while tending her nest.

Dogs and children should avoid entering the water in known alligator waters. While alligators tend to be intimidated by the presence of an erect human, a dog or small child splashing in the water may be looked upon as prey. In a recent tragedy, a three-year old child was playing in shallow water with his dog. Investigating officials theorize that a large alligator came forward trying to get the dog, but the animal hid behind the child, and the alligator killed the youngster.

If you do venture into the water, here's a rule of thumb that old-timers in Florida use: Never go in water beyond knee deep. A man can easily spot a gator hiding under water or lurking in grass in two feet of water, but deeper water may camouflage a sunken gator lying in wait.

If you venture into deeper water, make sure you're in a sturdy boat, and stay away from shores where vegetation may hide a large gator. And above all else, don't feed an alligator. You may not be attacked, but you'll surely create a dangerous situation for the next person.

How To Stop An Alligator Attack

If an alligator comes after you, run away. Gators make a furious initial run, but then usually stop to assess the situation. It's also a good idea to be armed in gator country. Surprisingly, pepper spray works well on gators. One man, who was attacked by a large alligator that latched onto his leg and was pulling him into the water, sprayed the gator in the face with pepper spray. The alligator released the man's leg and splashed crazily back into the water. The man was able to save his life, but gangrene set in and he lost the injured leg.

Alligator trapper Ray Ginn also noted that alligators don't like to be hit on the top of the head. Ray often works with the state of Florida to procure alligator eggs from nests. When the aggressive female charges, Ray told me that he just bonks her on top of the head with a long length of PVC plastic pipe, and that subdues her.

If you travel through gator country, plan to carry a six foot club or length of PVC pipe. If a gator corners you, charges or gets too close, whack it on top of the head, and it should retreat.

ALLIGATOR QUICK-CHECK LIST

How To Avoid Alligators

1. Do not feed alligators. They'll continue looking to you, or at

you, for more food after the snacks are gone.
2. Stay away from known alligator areas.
3. Avoid mud & grass mounds where a female gator may be guarding her eggs.
4. Avoid swimming in deep water near gator lairs.
5. Avoid grassy river banks or water vegetation where gators hide.
6. Avoid wading in water deeper than the knees.
7. Avoid wading while fishing with your catch on a stringer connected to your belt. The splashing fish may attract an alligator.
8. Keep pets and small children out of the water in areas where alligators roam.

How To Stop An Alligator Attack
1. Run away. Most gators will stop after their initial rush.
2. If charged or cornered by an alligator, hit it in the head to make it retreat.
3. If you are armed with a pistol, shoot an oncoming gator only if you feel your life is in immediate danger. Shoot for the head.
4. If you are armed with pepper spray, blast the oncoming gator in the face when it gets within 30 feet.

A mature wild boar may weigh 400 pounds and carries a wicked set of razor sharp tusks. They are shy creatures that hide in thickets, but a cornered or startled boar may charge. (Photo courtesy John Higley.)

CHAPTER TEN

The Wild Boar

Wild boars are feral descendants of domestic stock that roam the timbered ridges along the southeastern seaboard states, the Ozark Mountains and the thickets of California. They can weigh upwards to 500 pounds. They're also ill-tempered and carry a wicked set of razor sharp tusks that can be used with lethal effectiveness on an adversary.

Californian bowhunter Cliff Dewell found this out when he entered a dense thicket while trying to get a finishing shot at a 350-pound boar that he'd just wounded with an arrow. The animal charged and Cliff turned to run, but he had only taken three strides before the boar was on him.

The beast ripped a huge gash clear to the femur bone in the back of his leg and knocked him to the ground. Cliff began kicking with his feet to push the slashing beast away, but his legs became inoperable after being severely gashed many times by the enraged boar.

In the midst of this very desperate situation, Cliff remembered reading about how victims of grizzly bear attacks who played dead were able to stop a grizzly from attacking further. Cliff curled into a ball and stayed motionless. The boar continued to push at him, but it did not rip at his inert body with its tusks. The boar finally left, but Cliff was bleeding profusely from a gashed femoral artery. Cliff's partner applied a tourniquet and ran for help.

It took two and one-half hours for a lifeflight helicopter to arrive, during which time Cliff was able to relax the tourniquet three times to allow blood flow to the leg, but each time blood spurted from the slashed artery. By the time the helicopter arrived, Cliff had very nearly bled to death. It took nine days of intensive hospital care to pull him through.

How To Avoid A Wild Boar

Wild boars are secretive animals that are instinctively fearful of humans. In addition, lions and bears prey heavily upon smaller pigs, so a wild boar's immediate reaction to any suspicious sight or sound is to flee to dense cover. The problem arises when a wild boar is startled at close range with no time or avenue for retreat.

That's exactly what happened to Dan Homer when he emerged from an oakbrush thicket and dropped into a gully. He surprised a large wild boar twenty yards away at a waterhole. The startled pig squealed and charged. Fortunately for Dan, the boar had a bad front leg, probably injured in a fight with another boar, and Dan was able to scurry out of the gully before the pig got to him. As soon as the immediate threat was removed from the boar's sight, the animal swapped ends and ran the other way.

From the above incident, it is obvious that the best way to avoid a wild boar is to make a lot of noise, allowing it plenty of time to escape. You should also never approach a wild boar, even if it is aware of your presence. Wild boars are always fighting among themselves for breeding or feeding rights, and a boar that appears amiable may in fact be wounded and unable to flee at your sight — but it will charge if you move too close. A sow with piglets should especially be avoided because female wild pigs are very protective of their young.

Sportsmen who hunt wild pigs are attacked and injured every year when they follow a wounded boar into a thicket. If you wound a boar, allow a few hours for the animal to die. Never go into a thicket alone without a gun or pepper spray to thwart an attack. Cliff Dewell's horrific experience should stand as a sobering reminder to every sportsmen about the dangers of following a wounded wild boar too soon into a thicket without adequate backup.

How To Stop A Wild Boar Attack

A sudden rush by a wild boar can be stopped by shooting it in the head with a pistol. Pepper spray also works very well to turn an attacking boar. If a tree is nearby, you can climb it to escape a charging boar, and you need climb only about six feet above the ground to escape those tusks. If no large tree is available, try to get a large bush or small tree between yourself and the charging pig. A boar's charge is usually very fast, but short-lived. If a boar can't get at you the first time it lunges, it may break off the assault and then flee.

And as we learned from Cliff Dewell's experience, a victim of a boar attack who can't get the slashing animal off him might try playing dead, thereby posing no further threat to the boar.

An experienced boar hunting guide also mentioned that if a wild boar attacks a man and has him down, his partner can stop the attacking boar by grabbing it by the hind legs and pulling them up and off the ground and backward away from the downed victim. A wild boar is helpless without its rear legs under it, and the pig should become frightened and run off.

WILD BOAR QUICK-CHECK LIST
How To Avoid a wild Boar

1. Make lots of noise to give a wild boar time to escape.
2. Stay away from thickets where wild boars may be living.
3. Avoid an obviously injured boar.
4. Avoid a sow with piglets.

How To Stop a Wild Boar Attack

1. Climb a nearby tree to escape an oncoming boar.
2. Run away. A wild boar often will break off a charge from a fleeing human.
3. If you have a pistol, shoot the charging boar in the head.
4. If you have pepper spray, blast an oncoming boar when it gets within 20 yards.
5. If a boar has you down, play dead. The boar may quit slashing and move off.
6. If a boar has another person down, grab it by the hind legs and lift them off the ground.

Coyotes have rapidly expanded their range and now inhabit much of the East Coast. In suburban areas where they are protected, they quickly lose their instinctive fear of man and sometimes become brazen.

CHAPTER ELEVEN

The Coyote

There have been hundreds of millions of dollars spent to eradicate the coyote in the United States. Extensive private, state and federal control projects have used traps, guns and poison to eliminate this wily species. It has been all wasted money and effort. Today, there are more coyotes than ever, and this smaller cousin of the wolf has spread from the West all the way to the East Coast.

Coyotes also have a very unique biological reproduction system. When the coyote is plentiful, a female will have a litter of only a few pups. But when decimated, coyote litters shoot up to a dozen or more pups. In addition, the coyote is extremely adaptable. Unlike the grizzly, which needs wilderness, or the alligator that needs a warm swamp, the coyote is at home in the Arizona desert, a north Idaho mountain, or the hedge between two elegant homes in a New Jersey subdivision.

One problem concerning coyotes is the disdainful opinion most humans have of this wild dog. A coyote is not a quivering ball of fear that eats food scraps along a highway. It is a highly efficient predator capable of taking down full grown deer and aggressively defending itself. It's also an opportunist, and it will prey upon anything that is edible, including garbage, cats, dogs, or a child. The increase in coyote range and numbers, combined with civilization creeping into rural areas, has created a skyrocketing coyote problem.

If all that wasn't bad enough, eastern migrating coyotes have mated with feral dogs and produced a large hybrid called a coydog. The average adult coyote may weigh 35 pounds, but a coydog will weigh up to 50 pounds, and there have been reports of coydogs exhibiting very little natural fear of man in several eastern states.

How To Avoid A Coyote Attack

Normally, coyotes are extremely shy creatures with an almost hysterical inbred fear of man. No doubt, this comes from hundreds of years of massive extermination efforts. However, a coyote is quickly habituated toward humans if it becomes apparent that no harm will come to it. And a coyote that loses its fear of a human will soon begin to look upon humans with an opportunistic eye.

This is readily apparent in Yellowstone National Park where coyotes are protected and often fed by tourists. Occasionally, a lone hiker or skier is set upon by coyotes and bitten severely, Fortunately, no deaths have occurred — yet. That hasn't been the case in suburbia, where a few deaths of babies and children have been attributed to coyotes.

Recently in Cape Cod, a housewife rushed to her kitchen window and was horrified to see a coyote dragging her screaming three year old son into the bushes. The woman ran out and beat the coyote off, but it circled and tried to get at the older daughter, who had climbed to the top of the swing set.

The key to keeping coyotes away has always been to put fear of humans in them. But remember, these are very cunning animals. A scarecrow or firecrackers will quickly produce a shrug from these highly intelligent animals. Deadly force is the only method that I know of to keep coyotes at bay. In areas where coyote hunting is done, a coyote is usually just a brown blur at the sight of a man because it has learned that death awaits anywhere humans are found.

In an urban subdivision, it would be ludicrous to allow indiscriminate shooting because of the human safety hazard. However, a professional coyote hunter would keep the natural fear in the coyotes just by occasionally picking one off. I realize that a lot of folks don't like the idea of killing animals, but at times, it's best even for the animal species to administer this type of adverse conditioning.

There is a world of difference between the coyote that lives among the upscale homes in Cape Cod, and the coyote that is fair game outside the city limits. One is a brazen hunter, while the other is a brown blur.

To keep your home area free of coyotes, remove heavy undergrowth near your backyard. Coyotes don't like to be seen, and they'll avoid trotting through open areas, especially if they have a healthy fear of man. Of course, these coyotes move close to homes because of the availability of easy food. Remove those attractions that draw in birds, squirrels and rabbits, and you will have removed at least half of the attraction for the home-seeking coyote. Also, keep your garbage secure because a coyote will gladly eat putrefied food. In addition, it is a good idea to install a five foot high fence around the children's play area. A determined coyote can still get over it, but not easily, and it will give the kids enough time to flee.

I also firmly believe that a can of pepper spray stored in a safe place in the backyard is a great safety device just in case a brazen coyote should approach the kids. A blast of pepper spray will also furnish a fiery dose of adverse conditioning to an aggressive coyote, and that critter will probably never approach a human again. Coyotes are extremely fast learners.

How To Stop a Coyote Attack

Coyotes are very opportunistic, but they like the odds to be in their favor. A coyote may attack a child, but will usually be intimidated by an approaching adult who waves his or her hands and yells threateningly.

If a tree is nearby, a person who is confronted by an aggressive coyote should climb to safety. A car hood will also get you out of reach of a coyote. While you're doing this, make lots of threatening noises. It usually makes the coyote break off its attack.

Ultimately, a lethal weapon is the surest way to stop a

coyote attack. Any caliber pistol is enough to stop an attacking coyote. Often times, a few shots in the air are enough to unnerve a brazen coyote. Pepper spray also works very well against coyotes. A blast of red hot pepper in a coyote's snoot will surely give it a strong dose of adverse human conditioning.

COYOTE QUICK-CHECK LIST
How To Avoid A Coyote

1. Remove underbrush from around the house to discourage a coyote from sneaking through it.
2. Remove bird and animal feeders from around the house to keep away small birds and mammals that a coyote might sneak close to a house to catch.
3. Keep garbage cans secured so that coyotes aren't scavenging from them.
4. Encourage a professional predator hunter to safely eliminate a few coyotes periodically to keep a healthy fear of humans instilled in the local coyotes.

How To Stop An Attacking Coyote

1. If a coyote is attacking a child, run at the coyote while waving your arms and yelling. This should unnerve the coyote.
2. Climb a tree or jump onto a car hood to escape an attacking coyote.
3. Keep pepper spray in the backyard in a safe place for use if a coyote should enter the back yard. Instruct your children how to use it.
4. If you are armed with a pistol, fire a few rounds above the coyote's head. If the coyote continues forward, shoot it.
5. If you are armed with pepper spray, blast the coyote in the face when it charges within 30 feet.

CHAPTER TWELVE

Defending Against Rabies

Even in this enlightened age of great medical breakthroughs and scientific achievements, rabies continues to strike fear into the world. Unlike some Old World diseases which have been eradicated, rabies is still churning out a dizzying death toll. Upwards to 50,000 people throughout the world die a torturous death annually from rabies.

Not only is it a hideous disease and horrible way to die, but the manner in which it is transmitted also lends a macabre touch to an already dreadful malady. Rabies is transmitted by the bite of an infected animal. Literally anyone who is bitten by a dog, cat, bat or person must immediately deal with the haunting possibility of having been infected with rabies.

Rabies is nothing more than the condition that results from the introduction and proliferation of a specific virus into a human body. In man, this disease results in a severe inflammation of the brain or spinal cord (encephalomyelitis) associated with the invasion of these tissues by the rabies virus. Unfortunately, this condition is virtually always fatal.

However, rabies is not an incurable disease if identified and treated soon enough, and the nature lover who fully understands how this disease is transmitted, and how it affects a human body, stands an excellent chance of making a full recovery. The key here is to understand how the disease works and where it comes from. But most importantly, how to avoid it.

The History Of Rabies
Rabies has been around a long time. Outbreaks of this

disease have killed hundreds of thousands of people through the ages of recorded history. The rabies virus was first isolated by Louis Pasteur, who also created the first anti-rabies vaccine, but it surely existed long before that, though its effects were misdiagnosed as other diseases ranging from the plague to insanity. Historic records note the rabies disease as early as 1500, with continued and increasing recordings through the 1700's. Significantly, reports of rabies in the New World proved that rabies was not just a disease endemic to Europe.

The twenty-year period after the Napoleonic wars was especially bad for rabies in Europe. Foxes were initially infected, and they spread it to domestic animals such as horses, pigs, cows, cats and dogs. Many thousands of people also died after being infected by this disease.

Today, rabies has been eradicated from England, but much of the rest of the world is still burdened by it. Third World nations are especially effected. India alone reports about 15,000 deaths annually, but scientists wonder if many rabies cases in the backcountry are being missed.

In North America, the rabies virus continues to be spread by a host of carriers. Intense study and great gains in recent years have been made to eradicate and treat this disease to save humans infected by it. The unfortunate news is that today, rabies continues as a bothersome disease that infects hundreds of people each year, with a few deaths resulting.

How The Rabies Disease Works

An infected animal carries the rabies virus in its body fluid, and usually transmits it in its saliva when biting a victim. Once the rabies virus is introduced into the body, it enters a short incubation period whereupon it multiplies and then begins moving through the nervous system upward toward the brain. Once inside the brain, the virus begins to flourish and severe inflammation of the brain occurs. At this stage, rabies is virtually 100 percent fatal to humans.

Rabies Madness

The madness associated with rabies is due to the fact that one of the first brain sections affected is the limbic system, which controls emotions, aggression, arousal and sexuality. As the virus inflames the limbic, a victim begins to act moody, then gaily, then irritably, then angrily, then back to moody — until the patient is reduced to a raving lunatic (which is exactly what rabies was often misdiagnosed as).

Early Medical Help Cures Rabies

There are rabies vaccines and serums available to counteract the rabies virus, but these treatments work only in the early stages of rabies infection, before the virus proliferates and begins to move through nerves. For that reason, it is imperative to begin anti-rabies medication as soon as possible after being exposed to this disease.

One California woman, who was bitten by a bat, waited for forty-four hours until the tested bat came back positive for rabies. It was too late. Though immediate and intense anti-rabies treatment was begun, she died. As a result, medical experts now mandate that anyone who is bitten by a wild animal should begin rabies treatment immediately. This simple edict has saved untold lives.

Rabies Incubation Period

Rabies undergoes a slow process of gaining strength within a human body before it begins its deadly journey toward the brain. This is called the incubation period. This time period may vary from less than a week to two months or more. It depends largely on two things: How much initial rabies virus was transferred to the victim, and where the virus entered the body.

A scratch would allow a very limited number of the rabies virus to enter the body, while a vicious attack by a rabies-mad dog, including multiple bites, would introduce a much greater number of the virus.

The closer to the brain the virus enters the body, the

shorter distance it has to travel to get to the brain. A victim who was bitten on the neck or face may have only a week before the virus arrives at the brain, while a human bitten on an extremity, such as a foot, may have a month or more before the first signs of rabies appear.

Initial Signs Of Rabies

An untreated person who was unknowingly infected with rabies will probably show the first signs of rabies as a vague feverish illness. A feeling of being generally unwell, along with a loss of appetite, headache and other aches and pains, weakness, tiredness — sounds like the flu, doesn't it? Which is exactly what untreated rabies is often misdiagnosed as in its early stage.

These early symptoms soon are replaced by a feeling of tension, a sense of foreboding, depression, nightmares, inability to sleep and a lack of concentration.

The above symptoms are typical of many human conditions and hardly can be attributable solely to rabies. However, one more condition will emerge that is very rabies-specific. The victim feels a strange sensation radiating from the wound area, which has often already healed. Numbness, tingling, itching, coldness, burning, stabbing pain, trembling of the limb, and general weakness at that location should alert anyone that rabies may be the culprit.

The problem here is that, with the wound already healed, a physician may be baffled, especially if the wound had been small and no scar tissue shows. But a healed scar should be an immediate warning to any medical personnel that rabies could be behind this mysterious ailment. Unfortunately, patients are often shuttled off to ear, eye, nose or throat specialists, when they should be getting intensive rabies treatment.

Hydrophobia

Hydrophobia is Greek for "Dread of Water." This is a horrible symptom of rabies found only among human rabies victims. Animals do not experience hydrophobia. A rabies patient suddenly feels an overpowering craving for water, but when water is brought up to the lips, the patient recoils in horror. The head is jerked back, arms thrown out, and violent muscle spasms affect the entire body.

Patients therefore try hard to avoid water until their thirst is unquenchable, but when water is brought to them, they react with uncontrollable fear. Any liquid taken in is spat or gurgled out of the mouth, with vomiting followed by cries of alarm and the patient clutching at his throat.

These struggles of hydrophobia increase in frequency and intensity to the point where they occur spontaneously without the introduction of water. The patient then begins to become even more unruly and unmanageable, often jumping out of bed and running around like a madman, aggressively attacking anyone in his path. Now we know why much of the world still fears rabies.

Two Forms Of Rabies

Rabies symptoms can take on two forms in both man and animals. The first is called furious rabies, and the second is called passive, or dumb, rabies. In the most common form of rabies, furious rabies occurs when the brain is inflamed. In the less common form of passive rabies, the spinal column is affected. It is very important to understand that this deadly disease can occur in these two forms, so that a person does not misdiagnose a rabies infected animal.

Furious Rabies

Hydrophobia and madness are forms of furious rabies, so named because of the attack on the limbic section of the brain that controls such emotions. The majority of rabies victims will show signs of furious rabies, meaning that the virus has affected the brain. Besides aggressive actions, salivating, sweating and uncontrolled urination also result.

Passive Rabies

Passive rabies may actually be more dangerous that furious rabies. At least when you see a human or animal acting crazily, you know that something is very wrong, and the rabies connection is sure to occur to most observers.

Not so with passive rabies. Its victims at first experience classic flu-like symptoms of headache, nausea and cramps. But then numbness begins to affect the limbs and profuse sweating follows. At first, the victims are fully conscious, but eventually become delirious and comatose.

Most victims of passive rabies do not experience hydrophobia. They become listless and appear sad and depressed. In animals, the only time they tend to snap is when handled. This form of rabies carries great potential to be transmitted to someone who finds an animal lying quietly and appearing very sad. A human's first impulse is to console the animal, thinking it is either lost of has been separated from its mother. And, of course, we can't blame any animal who may nip a human because we figure the poor thing was just scared. Instead, it was in the latter stages

The skunk is a major carrier of rabies in certain areas of the West and East.

of passive rabies, and it just transferred the virus to the person it bit.

How Rabies Is Spread

Rabies can be spread by any warm blooded animal, but the primary spreader of rabies is the dog. Over 90 percent of all rabies cases in humans resulted from dog bites. And here are a few chilling statistics about dog bites. One half of one percent of the entire population of the U.S. is bitten by a dog each year, and it rises to 10 percent for children between two to ten years old. For this reason, it is critically important to make sure that any dog who bites a human is immediately captured and tested for rabies.

Depending upon the region of the country, rabies is transmitted and kept alive within certain species of wild animals. In the eastern U.S., the fox is the main carrier of rabies. In the South, raccoons are increasing in numbers and have become the principal carrier of rabies. In the West, the main host is the spotted skunk. In fact, old-time cowboys call it the "phobey cat." In the Rocky Mountain states, the striped skunk and ground squirrels are the wild animals most affected. In the Southwest, bats are the main carriers of rabies.

Though any number of wild animals are capable of spreading rabies, the skunk, raccoon and bat are the principal culprits in North America. That's because they tend to live in closely packed environments. In suburbia, overpopulations of raccoons and skunks congregate in populated neighborhoods nightly to scrounge for food, and the incidence of rabies infection among these species increases in proportion with their numbers.

Bats are especially dangerous as a host for rabies. These flying animals all flock together in tightly entwined bat roosts, where fighting with needle sharp teeth is common. In Central and South America, where vampire bats are common, they cause a heavy rabies-born economic loss to ranchers. It is estimated that upward to a million cattle die annually from rabies passed on to them by the bites of these blood sucking bats.

The one ray of sunshine concerning bats is that much of the

current knowledge and understanding of rabies has come from scientists who have studied bats in caves. But it came at a steep price. Some of these people contracted rabies and died, even though there were never bitten by a bat. Then a veterinary scientist contracted rabies and died after grinding up a rabid bat's brain for testing.

Scientists who studied the cave floor below the nesting bats were horrified to find a multitude of rabies spores on the floor and also floating through the air. Ultimately, scientists discovered that rabies could be contracted by several other methods besides a bite. Any mucus membrane, such as eyes, mouth, tears, saliva, sputum which came in contact with a rabies spore floating in the air near an infected animal could be used as a vehicle for the introduction of the rabies virus into a human.

HOW TO AVOID RABIES
Vaccinate Your Pets Against rabies

Since dogs are the main carriers of rabies to humans, it makes sense to insure your dog is free of the virus. A dog rabies vaccine is cheap and 90 percent effective to ward off rabies in a dog. This simple act will not only save your cherished pet from a horrible death, but it may also save human lives by removing your dog from the vicious rabies cycle among the canine family.

Be Aware of Rabies Symptoms

As you can see from the above literature, rabies is not a simple disease with apparent symptoms. It takes learning and studying to understand the dangers and causes of this disease. After you have a good grasp of the what, when, where and how of this disease, pass it on to your loved ones, especially children, because they are most prone to mistake the unnatural actions of a rabid animal as funny, cute or attractive.

Avoid All Wild Animals

Wild animals are wonderful to watch, but they should always be viewed at a distance. Any wild animal that appears uncharacteristically friendly, sad, lost or begins to approach a person — should be viewed with suspicion! These are unnatural actions for a wild animal because it should retreat or run away from a human. This is especially important for children to understand. That little raccoon sitting sadly in the back yard is sure to bring a gleeful response from a child who has been taught that raccoons are cute, cuddly animals — and now this raccoon in the back yard is proving it! Any animal acting in this manner is sick. It may not have rabies, but it certainly has some other sickness that could be equally dangerous to a human.

Avoid High Risk Rabies Areas

A few years ago, two cave explorers entered a cave where bats were nesting. They didn't stay long. Unfortunately, it was too long. They contracted rabies from airborne spores and died a few

In the South, the overpopulated urban raccoon is the main carrier of rabies.

weeks later. If you want to explore caves, stay away from those areas where bats are roosting.

Animal dens where cute little fox cubs are frolicking is another place to avoid. Also, the urban overpopulation of skunks and raccoons has brought the rabies problem right into heavily populated neighborhoods. Live trap, or eliminate, these backyard pests to lessen the chances of a rabid animal outside your home.

Avoid Strange Dogs

If a strange dog shows up at your home, call the animal control people. Let them feed and take care of it. They're best qualified to check it for rabies and then find it a new home. Many people are bitten by rabid dogs that they thought were just friendly, lost pooches who wandered onto their property.

How To Respond To An Animal Bite

Any animal, be it a dog, skunk, coyote or bat that approaches a person and bites him or her should be suspected of having rabies. At the moment of the bite, a time clock has begun, and it is imperative to accomplish several things immediately. Most importantly, the animal that did the biting should be captured, and authorities should be notified to have it tested for rabies. It is critically important to find out as soon as possible to verify this condition.

Next, any wild animal bite victim should be referred to a hospital, and rabies treatment should begin even before the animal rabies tests come back. There have been too many tragic stories of people finding out too late that the animal that bit them was rabid. And do not rely on a visual observation to determine if an animal is rabid. As noted previously, not all rabid animals react with the classic "Mad Dog" symptoms.

How To Avoid Being Bitten By a Rabid Animal

Often times, an animal will show all the classic signs of being rabid. It is an aggressive, slobbering beast snapping at anything within reach. You should do everything to avoid being bitten by this animal because the sad fact is that a small percentage of rabies victims die no matter how much help they receive.

If a possibly rabid animal approaches you, climb a tree, jump onto a car roof, even into the water to escape the charging animal's attack. A rabid animal's attention span is very short, so if it cannot bite you after a few attempts, its madness will send it scurrying elsewhere.

If you have nowhere to escape, blast an oncoming animal with pepper spray. Don't just give it a small shot, either. In this situation, it would be best to render such a beast inoperable to save other people from being bit. There have been many instances of rabid animals biting a dozen or more people before they finally collapsed or were captured. After your safety is assured, and the animal has run off, immediately call authorities and alert them that a possible rabid animal is on the loose.

Conclusion

The incidence of rabies is low in America. You may spend many years in the outdoors without encountering a rabid animal, but the fact remains that rabies is found in host animals throughout the United States and is even increasing among certain overpopulated animals. That's why it is important to understand the disease, know how to identify it, and then know how to deal with a rabid animal or a resulting bite. It could save your life.

RABIES QUICK-CHECK LIST

How To Identify A Rabid Animal

1. The animal begins to act moody, jumpy and seeks seclusion.
2. A dog stops barking and begins howling as if in pain.
3. The animal is intermittently friendly and aggressive.
4. Pupils are dilated and it intermittently charges and retreats.
5. The lower jaw droops down, making the animal salivate excessively.
6. The animal randomly runs around trying to bite anything in front of it, including metal, wood or people.

How To Avoid Contracting Rabies

1. Stay away from caves where rabid bats may nest.
2. Stay away from areas where animals are concentrated.
3. Remove backyard skunks and raccoons.
4. Stay away from any animal that acts peculiar.
5. Have your pets receive an anti-rabies shot.

How To Avoid Being Bit By A Rabid Animal

1. Climb a tree, car hood, or jump in the water to escape an obviously rabid animal.
2. Avoid being bit by a rabid animal as long as possible, even if you are cornered, because its attention span is short and it may scurry away if it cannot bite you after a few tries.
3. Spray a rabid animal with plenty of pepper spray to render it inoperable.
4. After the animal leaves, call authorities immediately and warn them about a possible rabid animal being on the loose.

How To Respond To An Animal Bite

1. Consider that any animal bite may carry rabies.
2. Capture the animal that bit you so that it can be tested quickly for rabies.
3. Go to a hospital immediately and begin rabies treatment if bitten by a wild animal, or a dog that could not be captured.
4. Alert authorities that you were bitten so they can take precautions to protect others in the area.

CHAPTER THIRTEEN

Making Your Home Safe

Statistics indicate that a disproportionate number of wild animal, snake and insect attacks occur at or near the home. These problem critters range from bears and lions in the West, to rabid skunks and raccoons in the East. In the South, rattlesnakes and alligators are a homesite menace, and in the Southwest, snakes and spiders often make the backyard a dangerous place.

It's not the critters' fault, either. When we move to the country, we should expect some interaction with these creatures. However, experienced rural dwellers have lived for many years among bears and lions and snakes and spiders without harm to themselves or their loved ones. They accomplished this admirable feat by examining their environment and then taking precautions to lessen the potential for accidental encounters with wild creatures.

The first chore is to learn which local wildlife have the potential to cause harm. It's then a simple matter of eliminating the conditions around the home that are conducive to their survival. Remove those conditions and the problem will also be removed. After all that, there is one final matter to attend to — education.

Children especially need to be taught at an early age which animals, snakes or spiders pose a threat to their safety. You don't have to scare them; just teach them how spiders live, where snakes like to hide, why lions may roam nearby, plus the fact that a wild animal acting docile and friendly should be avoided and never brought home because of the danger of rabies. I firmly believe that education and a casual, but constant, sense of awareness will spot 90 percent of all developing wild animal problems in advance.

The Proper Nature Lover's Philosophy

Living out here in the natural world is truly a privilege, whether you live way back in the woods, or just on the outskirts of town. Yet there tends to be an unnatural, and unhealthy, desire among the vast majority of rural newcomers to experience a heightened communion with the wild creatures out there.

Bird feeders are built, salt blocks are put out, fruit trees are planted, along with vegetable and flower gardens, plus a large lawn of Kentucky bluegrass. These are all fixtures meant to draw in wild animals so that the rural dweller can watch nature unfold out the kitchen window. However, they are unnatural, man-made things that create a mini-imbalance in nature's perfect cycle. But worse than that, these fixtures tend to draw wildlife toward a central meeting place — your home.

The result is more birds, more rabbits, more squirrels —

The idyllic urban home is nestled in the country without huge gardens, flower beds, fruit trees, bee hives, salt blocks or livestock. These extras unnaturally draw in wildlife and may cause conflicts.

all prime snake food. More insects proliferate among the shrubs and gardens, and more spiders hatch to prey on them. More deer crowd around the salt block out the back door, and more lions and coyotes lurk nearby to hunt them. More tasty fruit draws fall bears like a magnet. And, of course, sheep, llamas, horses, pigs, goats and chickens create an irresistible allure to every hungry predator in the area.

True oneness with nature requires the discipline to avoid acting, well, human! Instead of being a fixer and creator of monuments to one's self, it's important to fit into the natural world with as little impact as possible. In the end, there will be a sense of satisfaction and peace in knowing that you can function in harmony with the wild land and its inhabitants.

The Rural Home

The perfect country home is in the eyes of the beholder, be it a log home or ranch style house. But to be compatible with nature, your home should have as little impact on the environment as possible. Sure, a foundation and structure are necessary, along with a garage. But after that, do some thinking about how to best make these structures fit in with the natural scheme of things.

Many folks today live in serenity among the pines and oaks with the bare minimum of disturbance to the land. Little, if any, lawn grows. Instead, natural low vegetation is allowed to grow a safe distance from the home, with natural rock, gravel or wood bark surrounding the dwelling. Other than a graveled driveway, this setting is as natural, and ultimately, serene appearing as the proverbial little cottage in the woods.

Lion Proofing Your Home

As mentioned in Chapter Three, several very specific precautions should be taken to discourage lion activity near your home. First, remove all dense brush within fifty yards of your back yard. Lions are secretive animals and don't like to roam through open areas. A young lion that cannot sneak forward under cover may not have the courage to stalk forward after your favorite dog in the back yard.

Also, fight the impulse to put out salt to attract deer. This is a sure way to bring lions close to your house. If you must have a salt black, place it at least 300 yards away across an opening. You'll have to watch the deer at a long distance, but at least the lions will be far away, too.

A fence is another good idea, especially around the children's play area. Of course, no fence will keep a lion out, but it will slow one down, allowing your kids time to flee. I believe that it's also a good idea to keep a can of pepper spray handy in the kids' play area so that you, or a child, can grab it quickly if a desperate situation arises.

Vigilance toward disappearing pets is another way to protect your home against lions. Many lion tragedies began with a few cats or dogs suddenly coming up lost, followed by a lion sighting, followed by a big cat waiting outside someone's back door.

Bear Proofing Your Home

The backcountry subdivision where I live prohibits, to keep bears away, gardens or fruit trees. Simply put, bears have no reason to come near your home if you have no easy food available. Here's another clue for you to watch for in bear country. A bear passing through your property once is not a problem. That bear passing through again is a problem. That's because the bear has probably become attracted to some food source near your home.

My friend, Scott Matz, spotted a bear at the far end of his pasture one evening and thought it was pretty neat seeing a bear. The next evening, that bear was roaming outside his horse corral swatting at his barking dogs. The bear had become attracted to the horse oats in the barn. After many sleepless nights and several adrenalin-charged midnight bear encounters, the bear was live-trapped and removed, to eventually move back and harass some other rural dweller. The sad fact is that once a bear becomes habituated to human food, it can't stay away and is eventually killed.

Livestock in the country may attract large predators. Recently, a black bear killed a llama at a country ranch. The bear was then destroyed.

Skunk And Raccoon Proofing Your Home

Skunks and raccoons are drawn to rural homes because of food, mostly in the form of garbage. Both of these smallish animals are predators that can become aggressive when disturbed. They also wreak havoc with dogs and damage homes. If all that wasn't enough, these two animals are also the principal carriers of rabies, along with bats.

To discourage raccoons and skunks from coming around, construct a sturdy holding box for your garbage, and keep your barbecue safe inside the garage. If these pests persist, call a pest control specialist. These folks usually charge $50 to $75 per critter.

However, you'd be better off purchasing a live trap for about $40 and catching your own. Havahart Company makes a great live trap that is easy to use and easy on the animals. Just bait the trap with apples and you'll have Mr. Coon next morning. Take the coon to a faraway stream and release it.

Skunks are a bit more touchy. A skunk caught in a standard wire livetrap will surely stink up the countryside. Animal control suppliers now offer a special skunk livetrap that is made with black plastic instead of wire. After the skunk enters and is trapped inside, the black void keeps it docile, and you can pick up the trap and move the skunk a long way from your home. (See Appendix A for addresses of livetrap companies, but you might want to check out their availability at your local hardware store.)

Snake Proofing Your Home
Snakes need food, such as rodents; and shelter, such as den holes, rocks or wood. Take away those things near your home,

This mountain lion had to be destroyed after it climbed into a pen and killed a goat at a country home. Smaller domestic livestock at a country home sometimes draws bears, lions and coyotes. (Photo courtesy Kurt Wilson.)

and you will greatly reduce the snake problem. However, snakes may persist to be a problem, and you may need to find a more specific solution, like my friend, Joe Hintze, did in central Montana.

Joe moved to a small ranch with his wife and two little children. It had a nice lawn out back and nothing but pasture beyond, rising eventually to a low, rocky ridge 200 yards away. The very first evening, their idyllic Montana paradise turned into a nightmare!

Their Springer spaniel began barking furiously at something in the lawn near the kid's swing set. Joe found a two-foot prairie rattlesnake coiled and striking at the dog. Joe quickly killed it, but the dog was back barking within fifteen minutes. Yep, another rattler. Then another and another!

Joe's wife, Sherry, was terrified to go outside, and both parents feared for the kids' safety. Joe spoke to a nearby farmer about his snake problem, and the man recalled that he'd heard about a snake den being located in the rock outcrop above Joe's house. He gave Joe the name of a professional snake catcher, who was only too happy to help Joe.

Joe accompanied the guy to the den area and stared in horror at the huge ball of snakes at the mouth of a large hole under a rock ledge. The man caught thirty-six rattlers that first evening and sixteen the next day. Within three days, every snake was gone, and Joe's snake trouble disappeared as quickly.

A dog is a mighty handy sentinel for protecting children in snake country. Fido has the ability to see a small snake that a human may pass by, and those are the kind that bite kids because they're less visible.

Any parent in snake country should first make a cursory inspection of the playground area before allowing the kids to run outside in the morning. In addition, toys or boards should not be allowed to lay out overnight, where a passing snake might hide under after a night of hunting.

These simple rules are so effective that many residents in snake country never see a snake. A Florida friend told me that after taking the proper snake precautions, he's killed only one rattlesnake near his home in ten years — and this is in heavy snake country!

Spider Proofing Your Home

The vast majority of spider bites occur in or near dwellings. That's because spiders follow insects that seek out the dark places around and under home foundations, or under board piles in the back yard. Remove the insect prey base, and most spiders will leave for better hunting grounds.

In areas where the black widow and brown recluse are common, you should plan to insect bomb your home periodically, maybe once every two months. This same insecticide will also

The brazen urban coyote quickly loses its fear of humans if protected, and conflicts sometimes result. A professional coyote hunter will instill the natural fear of humans into local coyotes, and they will run away at the sight of man.

chase most of the spiders away.

Make sure your immediate backyard is immaculate, with no piles of boards or other items where a spider might hide. Mow any high grass along the playing area of the yard to keep spiders from hiding there. Remember, you'll never be able to remove all the spiders. You just want to move them back so that an accidental encounter in the backyard is unlikely.

However, all these precautions are fruitless if the crawl space under your home is a spider factory. I've crawled under some foundations and counted scores of black widow spiders hanging in webs. Plan to periodically bomb your crawl space to remove these unwelcome inhabitants.

In the home, keep piles of clothing and stacks of toys from gathering on the floor. Periodically spray dark closet corners and other areas where a spider and human might meet. Also, many humans are bitten by venomous spiders while in bed. For that reason, plan to spray under every bed and be very vigilant about checking under there for any sign of spiders.

Homes built in areas where wildlife have traditionally been, such as historic wintering areas for animals like the elk, create the potential for problem situations and homeowners need to consider what they must do if an encounter should take place.

EPILOGUE

Don't Take Chances!

Dale Burk, the publisher of this book and owner of Stoneydale Press, has been an outdoorsman all his life. When he was a kid growing up in the wilds of northwestern Montana, he spent days, even weeks, away from home in the most remote backcountry in the lower states. He hiked and camped and fished among grizzly and black bears and never had a problem.

When I asked him for a closing comment about staying safe in the wilds, he offered some sage advice. "My philosophy about going into the wilds has always been to avoid taking unnecessary chances. The more common sense rules of the woods, or stream, or trail that you break, the greater your chances of ending up in a predicament. If you avoid "iffy" situations, you should have few problems."

Yet every year, people pay the price for taking unnecessary chances. Hikers in Glacier National Park fall to their deaths because they take a chance and get too close to a spectacular waterfall. Photographers get attacked by elk and moose because they take a chance to get that great photo. And then there are the river floaters who shoot the rapids with kids aboard and no life jackets. As dangerous as we all know food in camp can be, folks still risk their lives by keeping food in their sleeping tents at night in grizzly country.

And we dare not forget Cliff Dewell's wild boar attack. Cliff broke one rule about not going in after a wounded wild boar without a self defense weapon, and he almost paid for that broken rule with his life!

This book has explained how wild creatures behave in the

wilds. It also details how to avoid them and how to stop them when they become aggressive. You now know the rules. If you follow them, you should have no problem with bears or lions or snakes or spiders. Ignore any of the rules, and your chances of having a problem increase.

Be a smart outdoors person. Better yet, be a safe one. Don't take chances!

Mike Lapinski

APPENDIX

Suggested Self-Defense Product Addresses

Videos

1. *Bear Attacks, Snowcrest Outdoor Products, 523 Main Street, Box 188, Stevensville, MT 59870 (1-800-735-7006).*
2. *The Fascinating World Of Alligators, Snowcrest Outdoor Products, 523 Main Street, Box 188, Stevensville, MT 59870 (1-800-735-7006).*
3. *The Fascinating World Of Predators, Snowcrest Outdoor Products, 523 Main Street, Box 188, Stevensville, MT 59870 (1-800-735-7006).*

Live Trap
Havahart Raccoon Trap
Krofick's Outdoor Supply
30 Lightcap Rd.
Latrobe, PA 15650
1-412-537-7923

Skunk Trap
Mitlyng Development
Box 43W
Darwin, MN 55324
1-800-298-8727

Snake-Proof Boots & Chaps
Cabela's
One Cable Drive
Sidney, NE 69160-9555
1-800-496-6329

UDAP Pepper Spray
13160 Yonder Road
Bozeman, MT 59715
1-800-232-7941

Self Defense For The Nature Lover

Additional copies of *Self Defense For The Nature Lover* can be obtained from many bookstores, sporting goods stores, other outlets, or directly from the publisher at Toll Free Number 1-800-735-7006, or by writing the address listed in the front of this book. Other books by Mike Lapinski are also available, including his highly acclaimed all-color, large format book on the wapiti (American elk) titled *The Elk Mystique*. Please call or write for a complete listing of these and other books on the outdoors, wildlife and historical reminisce available from Stoneydale Press.